GW00838488

THE HAMMER & THE PULPIT

THE HAMMER & THE PULPIT

BARRY F HANNANT

XULON PRESS

Xulon Press
2301 Lucien Way #415
Maitland, FL 32751
407.339.4217
www.xulonpress.com

© 2020 by Barry F Hannant

All rights reserved solely by the author. The author guarantees all contents are original and do not infringe upon the legal rights of any other person or work. No part of this book may be reproduced in any form without the permission of the author. The views expressed in this book are not necessarily those of the publisher.

Unless otherwise indicated, Scripture quotations taken from the Holy Bible, New International Version (NIV). Copyright © 1973, 1978, 1984, 2011 by Biblica, Inc.™. Used by permission. All rights reserved.

Scripture quotations taken from the English Standard Version (ESV). Copyright © 2001 by Crossway, a publishing ministry of Good News Publishers. Used by permission. All rights reserved.

Paperback ISBN-13: 978-1-6312-9984-1

Ebook ISBN-13: 978-1-6312-9985-8

TABLE OF CONTENTS

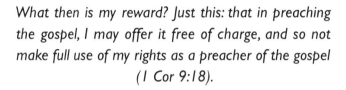

FOREWORD

What then is my reward? Just this: that in preaching the gospel, I may offer it free of charge, and so not make full use of my rights as a preacher of the gospel (1 Cor 9:18).

Bivocational Ministry: Back to the Future

WHEN I FIRST JOINED the Evangelic Free Church of America (EFCA) as the first director of Hispanic ministry, I reported that many Hispanic ministers were *bivocational*. One of the leaders for church planting ministry in the EFCA mentioned he didn't believe pastors and churches were serious if their pastor was not full-time.

I pointed out to him how numerous examples in the New Testament, including Paul, were bivocational ministers. I explained how at the turn of the century, ministers were bivocational. He conceded the point but also acknowledged it when he started understanding the context of many of our immigrants coming to America.

Bivocational ministry is increasing for many reasons, but one is the high bar of entry. Seminary is costly, and there is also the enormous amount of time the typical pathway takes. Even after that is accomplished, many with the training decide it is not for them. Typically, seminary training does not necessarily equip one for the diverse needs of America.

Clearly, the trend toward bivocational ministry is growing not just because of negative factors but also because of missional factors.

1. GATEWAY[1] helps train pastors for a fraction of the cost of standard training.

2. Bivocational ministry helps fulfill a person's call even if not optimally equipped.

3. Bivocational ministry allows one to live incarnationally in communities that might not welcome traditional ministers.

4. Bivocational ministry is becoming a viable option in post-modern society.

5. It helps start churches in under-resourced areas.

6. Invites congregants to believe that their work can be considered holy to the Lord.

7. It helps narrow the gap between theology and the practice of theology in the church.

While all of the above is true, we need to prepare our laborers with sufficient training that will equip them to raise up healthy churches capable of bringing transformation by good preaching of the Word of God and adequate skill training in church ministry.

Thus, GATEWAY Bivocational training meets a need: Theology and secular skill mentoring! GATEWAY has two commitments: Training to the level of earning a license credential in the EFCA, and assisting students to acquire tentmaking mentoring to be able to be self-sufficient in planting churches to serve all kinds of ministers for all kinds of churches.

Barry Hannant has modeled those two critical values from his work in Mexico and his work in San Antonio.

Thank you, Barry!

Alejandro Mandes- Executive Director of All People
Initiative for EFCA

ACKNOWLEDGEMENTS

I AM THANKFUL FOR the mentors and co-workers in my life, past and present, who believed in me and for pouring themselves into my life. My Uncle Carl once said, "Barry will be alright; he comes from good stock." My Grandmother Margorie gave me a place to call a studio in the basement of her home, where I was able to perfect my skills in oil and acrylic painting. Reverend Cory, the man who married Karla and I, was also an early mentor in biblical scripture. Milton, who took me under his wing, and for his family who co-taught me the skills of carpentry. For my good friend Mike Heller, who I went into battle with on many projects, and we were a great tag team. Thanks to Duane, Mary, and Mary D, who assisted in refining my artistic talent for the Gospel. For the men and women of the EFCA who became our handlers as we served overseas, and who also poured into us the need for authenticity in ministry. And for Alex, who sets scaffolding in place and allows his team to grow, run, and thrive in their lanes of influence. And most of all for my wife Karla, who the Lord gave me when we were both so young (married when we were eighteen and twenty-one years old). She has walked with me through it all, not only as a witness but also as a participant in her own right. In Mexico she worked at the DAYA Foundation, a home for marginalized girls. She poured her heart into the training and development of their character and taught them skills to use as young adults. They will never forget her.

INTRODUCTION

WHY WRITE A BOOK about bivocational ministry? Others before me, such as Tom Nelson or Hugh Halter, have done some in-depth commentary on this subject. I greatly appreciate their work, but have wanted to expound on the whole idea of a bivocational pastor from my own blue-collar perspective. My co-worker and boss, Alex Mandes, urged me to write about this topic because he knows the passion and skill I hold for this type of ministry. I had many wonderful teachers and worked with several masters of the trades during a spiritual awakening period in my life. As I point out in the following pages, I was raised in an un-churched home environment, but thanks be to God was saved at age nineteen, and had the scales removed from my eyes. I do, however, fully recognize the great job my parents did in creating a strong work ethic in me. The Lord had me right where He wanted me, working and studying His Word and perfecting both at the same time. Jesus said, "Follow me and I will make you fishers of men," and like him, I too have followed instructions from tradesmen and learned well as he did with his earthly father, Joseph. This is a book of ideas, and it's about being put to the test. Like famous artists of the sixteenth and seventeenth centuries who studied under a master, let me take you on a little journey and you just might discover how to build a house, or paint, or maybe even take your trade into the marketplace and share Jesus in a completely holistic manner, shoulder-to-shoulder with the novice, the master, and the people. Let's get started! The artwork in this book comes from my collection of personal drawings and paintings over the years. I always say, like the old adage, "A picture speaks a thousand words," so if my words don't tell the story, maybe the drawings will. Enjoy!

"I practice this type of ministry in the world because it expands the kingdom of God. It is the missional extension of the body into schools, offices, neighborhoods and work places in the community. BIVO is a holistic, natural return to a ministry that serves the body, mind and spirit."

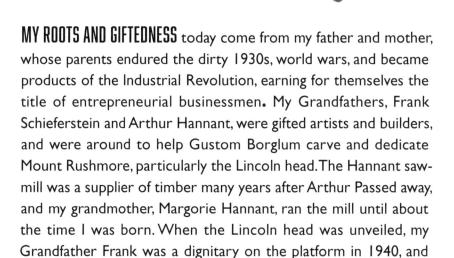

BIOGRAPHY

MY ROOTS AND GIFTEDNESS today come from my father and mother, whose parents endured the dirty 1930s, world wars, and became products of the Industrial Revolution, earning for themselves the title of entrepreneurial businessmen. My Grandfathers, Frank Schieferstein and Arthur Hannant, were gifted artists and builders, and were around to help Gustom Borglum carve and dedicate Mount Rushmore, particularly the Lincoln head. The Hannant saw-mill was a supplier of timber many years after Arthur Passed away, and my grandmother, Margorie Hannant, ran the mill until about the time I was born. When the Lincoln head was unveiled, my Grandfather Frank was a dignitary on the platform in 1940, and Arthur was there as well.

Dad moved our family to South Dakota from Texas in 1963, and growing up there we hardly ever darkened the door of a church except occasionally. Any understanding about God I had started forming at the age of eighteen or nineteen years old. Concepts of God in my teen years came from occasional Easter holiday atten-dance of church with my parents and grandmother. Being raised by secular parents in this decade meant doing chores around the house. Lots of chores, all the time, and you were expected to pull your own weight. There were weekly assignments consisting of washing dishes, cleaning the house, garbage removal, yard work, window cleaning and schoolwork. By the way, as noted by others who grew up in this era, we did walk several miles to school each way, and at times did so in inclement weather. There was no such thing as a cell phone either. We relied on our word and timing to be home by a certain time, period. While one could certainly grumble and resist, the training did help me understand the value

1

of a day's work and of the dollar. In fact, by age fourteen I was working at my first part-time job away from home making $1.25 per hour building burial vaults. My mother would take me to and pick me up from this part-time job during the summer. By the time I was able to pay for my first car (a 1955 Ford Custom), I was able to start my second job with Woolworths during my high school years. The $1.25 was saved and accrued to over $150 during the summer, and I was able to pay $75 for the car, and paid for insurance, my driver's license, and fuel.

Influenced by secular men and women, I remember my first spiritual longings developed from a biography of Michelangelo called *The Agony and the Ecstasy.*[2] As a young boy, Michelangelo was trained in the skills of marble carving and worked for priests and kings. But the early years of my youth seemed to be plagued by trouble with my parents. Maybe I was a handful, or maybe I was too much for my parents, but at one point it occurred to me to attempt to run away from home. This ended badly when I got caught in the next state over. Suffice it to say, by the time I was eighteen years old it was time for me to leave the nest, and it did happen when I went away for college at Yankton Art School in eastern South Dakota. There were a few opportunities to meet Christ followers on campus, but I ran with other crazy artists who kept talking about marijuana and acid, which thankfully I stayed away from for the most part. In the end, that place was not for me and I returned to Rapid City, seeking ways to use my artistic ability. By the time I met Karla, my future wife, the Holy Spirit was working to lead me to a life with Jesus.

Conversion

In 1973 one night, I met Jesus Christ in the forest on a road to a church camp. Just before my encounter with Jesus, I witnessed a beautiful worship of Him through song and prayer at Placerville

Camp in the Black Hills of South Dakota. Karla was engaged in this worship event and I was on a hill overlooking the little church in the forest. The back story is this: I had permission from my father to take his pickup truck and go visit Karla. He didn't know she was at this church camp, fifteen miles from Rapid City. The emotions inside me were overwhelming, not understanding the fellowship between believers, running scared from that scene in panic, I got my father's truck stuck in a ditch and continued by foot. On that two-mile gravel road back to the main highway, in the dark, I began talking to Jesus. Before long I was kneeling and praying for forgiveness and His help. The evening was not over yet! I approached the main highway with a new condition in my heart: Jesus was with me. But how to get home now? There were no vehicles and the hour was past time for my promised return home with my father's truck.

It was just then that a jeep was approaching, and to my surprise it was a fellow classmate, Rob Hanson. He stopped and said, "Hop in. I'll take you home." Rob was also visiting his girlfriend and we both seemed to be in a similar predicament. He was driving his father's Jeep and he was late getting home. We made our way back to town, and as we rounded the corner on a ridge above Stevens High School in west Rapid City, disaster struck! Literally, the steering wheel came off into Rob's hands and the Jeep plunged down into a ravine. We bailed out unscathed as the jeep hit a post at the bottom and came to a stop in good little dust-up. Now we were both going to have to walk home without our father's vehicles, and in the dark! I walked the next three miles wondering what would be waiting for me when I got home at 1:00 AM. But with Jesus in my heart, it did not matter anymore, but once again I had caused strife and problem with my parents. Dad booted me right out the kitchen door and was furious with me as he and my twin brother left in the 1965 Chrysler Newport to go get his pickup. I could not tell him what a heart change was going on inside me. Although he might have understood, Mom would not be

3

so forthcoming as she was at best an Agnostic in those days. And that is how it was – hard days and life full of tension, but the tide was turning in my favor.

A bible was handed to me a month later and I began to read, discovering key scriptures that corresponded with the time when Jesus came to me on Placerville Road. "If you declare with your mouth, 'Jesus is LORD,' and believe in your heart that God raised him from the dead, you will be saved" (Rom10:9). Later, as I was being discipled by the man who married Karla and I, the Reverend George Cory, this special verse was revealed to me: Philippians1:6, which assured me that Jesus would carry on the work in me He began, and that I could trust His presence in my life, for He would not forsake me or leave me.

That night I was saved, but it took several years of discipleship and Bible study to understand what my decision really meant – a life committed to Christ. Karla and I were married in 1975 and I was baptized in December 1986, making a public confession of faith in Jesus eleven years later.

The Bible opened my eyes to the Creator and the wondrous design of nature and God's beauty. God had equipped me with gifts like Bezalel (Ex 35:30) who had skills in all kinds of crafts and artistic design. I left art school for a career in construction and became a home builder, and later a builder of Churches. At this same time, I gained an opportunity to illustrate weekly sermons at a Lutheran church, then later at an Evangelical Free Church for several years. Becoming a carpenter served me well given my skill sets and ancestry. I continued to grow spiritually and developed a stronger appreciation for biblical application in building the kingdom of God (1Cor 3:10). My wife, Karla, had come to Christ as a young teen at a David Wilkerson Crusade. She also came from a family of carpenters and worshiped in a congregational church. From the time Karla and I started dating on through to early marriage years, we both attended and served in the First

Congregational Church. We understood our role and spiritual giftedness in God's kingdom, and He has used us and still does to this day.

Looking for better spiritual discipleship for our family, we joined an EFCA church planted in South Dakota in 1981, which is where I experienced the strongest spiritual growth period of my

life, apart from my missionary experience in Mexico. It was our time in the Dakotas when we understood the developing missionary journey, doing projects for pastors and missionaries in their homes and churches, and leading "junior church" at Rimrock EFC.

Before our marriage, at Yankton College my impression of the art world was they are all crazy (professors and students alike). It was Art History that caught my attention, as well as the many mediums from which one could produce art. But it did not seem like a viable career path, and my heart was being pulled in a new direction. God showed me a different path from becoming a commercial artist, and introduced me to Gospel art. Telling the Story with chalk art became an option when I met Duane Laughlin and Mary Doscher, which resulted in a trip to Wynona Lake, Indiana for a week. It was at the Christian Magicians conference where I was tutored by Gary Means, Dean Tueling, and other semi-retired pastors who were masters in the trade. Mary, a Godly woman, gave me her chalk easel after this and I began my version of twenty-minute storytelling for the next many years.

Self-Employment

We purchased our first home in Rapid City, before our marriage, making improvements and re-selling it for double the purchase price. The second home we bought was also a money-maker for building equity, and our first son Tarver was born before our move to Henderson, Nevada. The home in Nevada was lost to a period of formal unemployment, and our second son Justin was born prior to our return to Rapid City. The next home we purchased was a repossession. We got in for a $100 down payment and made major improvements to it. Karla began a licensed home day care that required more

space for the ten children she cared for. Soon our family moved to northeast Colorado where our oldest son was injured in an accident that challenged us greatly. But we also began another private business with crafts and artisan products. It was this self-employment that gave us the freedom to deal with the medical issues of our oldest son. It was a time of travel to Galveston, Texas and nearly six years of prayer battle for his life and health.

After moving to Colorado, our family endured a terrible accident (#1) that severely injured our oldest son, Tarver. At age fourteen he suffered electric burns on more than third of his body and eventually the loss of his left leg. This event was a trial by fire and included six years of burn treatment on Galveston Island in Texas. Many who knew our family said we held together through our faith, and even the doctors in Galveston agreed we were a strong unit. Perhaps I will devote more writing space about this experience another time, but we thank God today for entrepreneurial CAN-DO spirits during this trying period in our marriage. Becoming self-employed allowed us to deal with our son's serious injuries and care for our other son at the same time while earning a living. It was period in our lives that was both painful and emotional, but filled with grace.

We survived, and our sons Tarver and Justin grew into strong young men and began their own families. Tarver went to Western University in Oregon, and Justin went on to law school at Thomas Jefferson Law in San Diego.

In Lorenzo, Nebraska, I began Hannant Construction, and we still maintained B&K Crafts, traveling to various outlets selling our wares. We also employed friends, family and churchmen when preparing for a major showing in places such as Montana (Great Falls, Missoula, and Billings), Colorado (Fort Collins, Sterling and Denver), North Dakota (Bismarck and Fargo), and many townships in South Dakota.

The Calling

During a mission weekend in 2003 in Sidney, Nebraska, both Karla and I heard the Call to go full-time into missions as our two sons were entering their college and army years. We had already participated in many short-term trips to Mexico and Romania. Much like Samuel as a boy, we said to each other, "Did you hear that?" I asked, "What did you hear, Karla?" She said, "I heard a call to enter full-time into mission work." And I said, "The same calling came to me as well!" Almost a year later we filled out the applications and sent them to the home office of the EFCA International Mission. Our two sons and their wives were fully in agreement with the decision. But God had a plan to help us depart from Hannant Construction involving a terrifying accident #2 one week after we sent our applications into the EFCA Mission. The car accident broke my neck (4/5-6/7 vertebrae) and effectively removed the hammer from my hands for such a time.

I had already begun transitioning from custom-home work and light industrial projects into working for Brown Church Development Group[3] (BCDG), a church development company that needed superintendents to oversee projects around the region. The accident did not keep me away from the job sites, though. While at BCDG, I helped raise up churches in North Dakota (Bismarck), Nebraska (Omaha, Kearney, North Platte, and Sidney), and completed my last one for them in Dubuque, Iowa. We completed the building work in late August 2006, and by October of that year we arrived in Mexico City. Missionaries prepare for all sorts of situations, but preparing for a specific amount of time is crucial. The first time slot would be a short-term trip to an unknown area, requiring a week or ten-day adventure in which you give up your right to be comfortable. The BCDG time period typically is fourteen months, give or take, where the supervisor (and his family) are required to relocate to another township and make new friends. The third rail of time periods is going overseas for ten years or more and doing the same thing you did in the first two periods. My wife and I have experienced all three of these time periods. We also traveled 50,000 miles raising our support levels during a two-year period.

After the accident that broke my neck, there was a recovery period from surgery, and I healed quickly, opening the door for our next steps. What does not kill you will make you a better person. Oh, and by the way, it was a huge answer to prayer: God, how will you move us out of rural Nebraska and into a life of missionary service overseas? I know that is a cliché, but it's true in my case, so just an observation here and some advice: Don't ask God how He will do it because you might not want to know! We attended Candidate School and doctrinal review classes, and were accepted into the Mission. After two years of tentmaking, we arrived in Mexico (2005-2015) to engage in holistic ministry, planting churches, developing micro-enterprise ministries, and even serving at an orphanage for six years. Karla and I have journaled and kept records, photos, and tons of memories about this precious time in Mexico. People ask if it was dangerous, and we say sure it was, but it was also rewarding, beautiful, scary, unnerving, dark, joyful, educational, and all the other emotions known to man. There are a thousand things you can say are bad about Mexico, and there are a thousand things that are very good about it. Our entrepreneurial background helped us a lot, but our deep faith rooted in God's Word with the Spirit's presence carried us beyond just surviving. In fact, we thrived. You will read some of the adventures in this book, but perhaps more writing some other time will tell more about the amazing ten years we spent there.

Today we are involved with church planting and compassion ministry serving on the All People Team with the EFCA. I hold a Ministerial License in the Texas-Oklahoma District of the EFCA, was previously licensed in the Midwest District of the EFCA, and Commissioned to Ministry out of the Sidney EFC in Nebraska.

In San Antonio, I hold a General Contractor's license and am insured and bonded, able to pull permits and oversee construction. Church building is a passion of mine, but I've worked since 1972 in the trades, building more than 1,500 homes. I was a member of Union Carpenter Local 1780 in Las Vegas, and served eighteen months on the NTS (Nevada Test Range) during the Ronald Regan administration. My experience extends to drawing, painting, taping, wallpaper, cabinetry, concrete, architecture design and drafting, carpentry. and stonework (Ex 35:30-35).

As a bivocational missionary/pastor/carpenter, my experience and background serve me well to write on the topic of bivocational ministry, about which I'm very passionate.

THE MOTTO

I WAS BORN IN a Navy Seabee Base Hospital in Port Hueneme, California in 1954 with my twin brother, Bryan. My father was stationed there during the Korean War as a gifted machinist on a boat called the USS Norton Sound. Dad had the rank of Chief Petty Officer. After mustering out of the Navy shortly after our birth, Dad moved our family to Houston, Texas. We again re-located, this time to Rapid City, South Dakota in 1963 where my parents had their roots in the Black Hills.

Who are the Seabees? What can they do? What can they teach us today about work ethics and team building? The Navy Construction Battalion combines amazing efficiency, teamwork and reliability to build almost anything permanent or portable. With the Seabees, you may take on any number of important roles, each of which is in high demand in both the military and civilian sectors. Their mottos include "WE BUILD, WE FIGHT" and "CAN DO!" A career as a Navy Seabee can provide valuable training and experience in construction trades. Another of their mottos: *With willing hearts and skillful hands, the difficult is done at once and the impossible takes a bit longer.* The image of the Seabee is essentially an image of bivocational status representing a variety of skills, which some may call multi-tasking. The three legs of the worker bee present symbols of a weapon, a wrench, and a hammer. My intention for this book is to illustrate and demonstrate bivocational ministry using a hammer, the pulpit, and a passion for extending the reach of the gospel to those outside the church today. *The Hammer and the Pulpit* is not meant for using either one or the other, rather they complement each other and work in conjunction with each other, thus the name for this book. We know that the Scriptures are verbally inspired as God spoke through certain men moved by the Spirit but retaining our unique identity. We already have the mandate from Jesus to go and make disciples, so why not attempt a little MacGyver-style ability to accomplish the Lord's will?[4]

Indeed, the workload of a bivocational pastor is exhausting. It takes a dedication to detail, a self-starter attitude, and a grittiness demonstrated by armed forces personnel who fight for and defend our country. I never served in the mili-

tary, but many family members of mine have, including my youngest son Justin. This is a story about the training and developing of an individual to become a viable resource for his family and to expand God's kingdom on earth. It has been said there is nothing stronger than the heart of a volunteer. But not all volunteers are cut out for the rigors of bivocational ministry. One key way to be sure if a person can handle the discipline and refinement process is to squeeze, press, and challenge him a little bit. The potter chooses the lump of clay and then precipitates the clay to beat out all the air possible. I Corinthians 9:24-27 talks about this precipitate process in running a race, don't do it aimlessly, don't box as one beating the air, discipline your body, exercise self-control. When God gave Elijah

a trainee, a novice, a Timothy in Elisha, the young man was found tending a field with twelve pairs of oxen. When David was called into ministry, he was tending his father's sheep and was highly skilled with a sling. The pattern continues when Jesus chose his first disciples from the working class and not from the ivy-leaguers. The Lord sees the heart, which is a lot more difficult for us to do, and that's why we test and observe a person before continuing the training.

> Faith is never passive. It demands a response. It asks for a mission. It demonstrates the indwelling presence and power of the Holy Spirit. ~ Pastor Richard Wurmbrand

Why write this book?

Uneducated, common men astonished the Pharisees and Sadducees in the fourth chapter of Acts. The disciples were asked by what power or by what name did they do this? Here's Peter's response:

> Rulers of the people and elders, if we are being examined today concerning a good deed done to a crippled man, by what means this man has been healed, let it be known to all of you and to all the people of Israel that by the name of Jesus Christ of Nazareth, whom you crucified, whom God raised from the dead – by him this man is standing before you well. This Jesus is the stone that was rejected by you, the builders, which has become the corner stone. And there is salvation in no one else, for there is no other name under heaven given among men by which we must be saved (Acts 4:8-12 ESV).

The term *discipleship* is used so widely today it has become a phrase of generic meaning and not of a specific meaning and intent. Yes, as you ponder on its definition your mind may travel directly to its spiritual meaning and application. This term can be defined as teaching, training, equipping, releasing the laymen into service for the Lord. The word *discipleship* is critical in church and leadership development and is at the core what my book is all about, yet does not show up as a word so much in my writing. Similarly, with the term the *Trinity*, we see it weaving through scripture and recognize it as identifying one God three parts, but the word is found in broader sentences (Let Us Make, Let Us Do, as in Gen 1:26 and 3:22). In addition to Genesis 3:22, verse 23 sets the standard for our earthly lifespan: We are destined to work the ground from which we are made from via Adam.

An important question for any campaign, mission, or business model is "How do we measure success?" In disciple making I am suggesting we measure for success by first measuring, then measure often. You see, if we are training, teaching, sharing the gospel daily, then we are also taking a measure of the person whom we influence. At the very basic, fundamental level of carpentry, in order to facilitate transition from a rookie to a master, one must first be taught to measure, secondly to make a cut, and thirdly put the item into position, fitting it properly. Then we step back, observe, and take an accounting. If there needs to be any adjustments, then it will be yet another teachable moment for the master and student. Of course, the next steps of fastening systems, finishes, and presentation make for a deeper learning tract for the novice. At some point along the process, a student discovers his or her sweet spot. Practice makes perfect. But one important element of coaching a novice is to teach through example, such as stop doing something that is not productive. Practically speaking on the field, for instance, do not choke too far up on the hammer, unless your strikes are low-pressure taps such as fitting a piece into position. Use the head and the shank properly and practice a lot or you will miss the mark.

In an illustration from the world of a stone carver; it is said that even paving stones in Florence are works of art. Michelangelo spent considerable time choosing a marble rock from the Carrera mountains. Even after the huge stone arrived in his studio, he examined the fissures and colorations to make sure there would be no cracks in key areas of the work. The artist or coach has an image in his mind of the finished work. The correct tool is chosen to begin the removal of foreign product – stuff that will not complement the completed design and hinder the desired profile. Again, as I talk about precipitate and the process of beating the air out of clay, this is very similar. And of course, the potter selects various tools to mold, shape, even cut out or smooth the turning/spinning lump of clay. Then there is a final polish. Sometimes lard or pig fat was used to rub the stone to a sheen or low luster. But long before the chisel could be put to stone, there was the idea, the sketch, the temporary models, the measurements, and even the specific base of operation, where the diamond in the rough would be brought out and refined. We are being refined and matured but not in a vacuum, and always for a purpose (Gen 1:28-31). When man was first formed by the hand of God, the environment was already in place – a perfect studio where the new creation could glorify his maker in all that he does.

FUEGO

The word *fuego* in Spanish means *fire* or *flame*.

> "Therefore, since we are surrounded by so great a cloud of witnesses, let us lay aside every weight and the sin that clings so closely, and let us run with perseverance the race that is set before us" (Heb 12:1)

IN 2013 I ATTENDED a FUEGO conference with my wife in San Antonio, Texas. It was a joint conference with the Navigators at the Westin Hotel, and many Hispanic leaders were there. As I sat in a session whereRicardo Palmerin was speaking, a gentleman introduced himself to me. Troy was not his real name, but I will use it for this explanation. We began talking about our own personal training and upbringing, and Troy said to me, "My father was one of five brothers and he was the only one who took up carpentry, learning from his father. Today, my father is in a nursing home and he laments that he did not successfully pass on the knowledge of the trades he possessed in his mind." He did not have a "Timothy" or a disciple to teach and he was sad. Troy and I both lamented that there needs to be an awareness of this fact among strong believers in the Lord. We should teach our children what we know, and how we know it. It requires a holistic approach. It was our conviction we have something to learn from our masters and we should share what we ourselves have learned.

Then about a year later I was invited to attend a bivocational forum at the Denver Seminary with fellow Free Church pastors who were in one way or another practicing a bivocational approach in their respective ministries. No one from our group had a platform to speak. Don't get me wrong, it was good, I enjoyed Hugh Halter and his story. The voices we listened to did not exactly nail down my own belief and thinking pattern. And like my fellow EFCA pastors, we felt we could speak into this issue of bivocational ministry from our own experiences. Tom Nelson wrote a great piece called *Work Matters*[5] and as I absorbed his writing, again I realized how my perspective was one of a blue-collar angle and having the life knowledge of being a carpenter/pastor. That's why the title of this book is *The Hammer and the Pulpit*.

The other reason for this book, is to be the tip of the spear and blaze a trail into the future of Oikos, that is: of the look and appearance of the local body of believers. One important verse to

The Joy of ministry.
Phil. 1: 12-18

"IN GOD WE TRUST"
Early Americans called to be a land of the FREE

4-15-06

keep in mind (and I give many scriptural observations along the way) is I Corinthians 9:7. "Who serves as a soldier at his own expense? Who plants a vineyard without eating any of its fruit? Or who tends a flock without getting some of the milk?" I am reminded of the first worship service for Jesus, which was the Angels singing to the Shepherds tending to their flocks — oh yes, and it was *in the field*, not in a building we call a church today. The angel also told the shepherds there was a baby, the newborn Messiah, laying in a "manger." The manger is a spiritual symbol for a storehouse of nourishment, and we can go to the Lord anytime we feel hungry (Ps 107:9; Is 49:10). Workmen in the field worshiping the savior of the world and soon enough Jesus patterns his ministry around the common worker-servants. So, this is the direction we are headed

– a holistic, natural return to our roots in a small group called the "Way." It's a holistic approach that serves the whole body, mind, and Spirit.

I had wonderful multiple teachers who helped in developing my God-given talent and skill sets. And today is all about preparing for what is next in your timeline of becoming a mature believer, weening yourself from just milk like a baby to eating meat and potatoes. Be fruitful and multiply.

The gospel itself was originally given in a social context. The biblical writers did not speak in a social vacuum, and we don't read the word in a social vacuum. God wants to meet men and women in their own cultural and social situations. The gospel is able to incarnate itself in any kind of culture without losing its own identity. Why are so many Central Americans coming to the United States? Political refugees, no jobs, no hope of a better life in their own country see America is the land of promise – it appears to the world as a breadbasket. Remember, America was built in part by immigrants through divine guidance into a great Nation. In Latin America, values are changing. There has been a change of family, morals, and religion due to cultural shifts. The old church is no longer a haven for the old way of life in Central America or the USA. What institution is going to speak of love, justice, reconciliation, and peace in the name of the Lord Jesus Christ? The church has to be ready, always open to receive those who in times of social peace or social conflict are looking for spiritual help.

I learned and old lesson while serving in Mexico, one that resonated when I attended Fuego in San Antonio. There is a need for missionaries to teach – mission theology and praxis – a need to emphasize more than ever the humanity of Christ and holistic practices.

From a conference I attended in Latin America, where the topic was about the need for teaching, below are some of the needs mentioned:

- New Testament teaching on good works.

- The example of the first-century church in the area of social responsibility.

- The social implications of the gospel in relation to the dignity of women.

- The nature and purpose of human government.

- Our Christian behavior as members of the Civil Community.

- The biblical concept of labor and social justice.

- Peace as the result of the practice of justice.

- Love as the key word in our human relations.

- The present Lordship of Christ over creation and history.

- His final triumph over forces of evil in this world.

- The cosmic renovation as the final chapter in this redemptive program on earth.

Finally, the method of learning is accentuated when we *engage in a personal involvement* and prayerfully observe the novice. Below is how much the average person retains from different ways of taking in information:

1. 10% of what we read.

2. 20% of what we hear.

3. 30% by watching a demonstration.

4. 50% by combining #2 and #3.

5. 70% by combining #4 with writing out what you learned

6. 90% by using all of the above plus application and practice.

Acts 13:47 says, "I have made you a light for the Gentiles, that you may bring salvation to the ends of the earth."

IDENTIFY

What BIVO is not:

The term BIVO= bivocational ministry.

IT IS NOT A secular-orientated person or organization that is detached from a core value of bringing people to Christ. There are many who work two jobs to pay the bills, and though it appears as bivocational, this view is not purposefully supporting evangelical efforts. This book is intended to demonstrate how to use various skills to teach and train, to enter into community and have a positive holistic effect on the lost.

It can be *tentmaking*, a vocational skills program, to augment a pastor or missionary income, and most importantly bring Jesus into the marketplace and to common people. It can be an externship (outside the church) rather than an internship (within the church). I have heard of a recent trend to name this type of ministry " Co-Vocational," and that it might flesh out to be a percentage of work type of plan (25%/75%). Perhaps we can have another discussion on the merits of this title, but for my purposes – BIVO is defined differently.

Non-BIVO examples might be in tentmaking, which includes non- teaching positions where while in the employ of another, a service is provided. Any position of labor or skill where you can do the assigned task without training another person or novice. It can be on an assembly line, as a telemarketer, a temporary laborer in construction, seasonal positions, part-time farmers, or one-time services performed solo or in a group to supplement ministerial support.

BIVO is not a replacement for Traditional Church and is not suitable for a larger churches of more than 200. Even at a number like 100 souls in a congregation, a minister is called to intentionally focus on the needs of the flock or train a core group to meet the need. BIVO is a way to build a network and develop a core group to meet a basic need in the market place with spiritual fellowship for those who do not attend a church. One of the goals, therefore, is to foster and be a catalyst for church planting in unreached areas. Once the laymen are trained and equipped in a skill (GATEWAY for example) along with matters of theology and prayer, they can reproduce the model with on-going guidance. The BIVO pastor coach moves on but remains connected as an interim coach.

BIVO is not for the faint of heart! This concept of growing in knowledge and wisdom does not come strictly from a book or classroom. I have read books that rail against pastors with awesome bivocational skill sets and who are somehow minimized as second-class pastors because of this experience, and seem to be placed on a sub-level or become parachurch workers. What makes a successful pastor? Is there such a thing as first- or second-class pastors? I would argue that relationships guided by the Holy Spirit, mixed with skill and experience, become the "proving" and the "qualifying" that God does. Prior to his ministry years, Jesus grew in wisdom and stature and in favor with God and man (Mt 3:16,17; Lk 2:52). This is our biblical model of an effective, successful pastor, that is to say, a man enriched in theology and in good works.

I have wondered about the moment Jesus came up out the water after John baptized him. The heavens opened and Jesus saw the Spirit of God descending like a dove and coming to rest on him; and behold a voice from heaven said, "this is my beloved Son, with whom I am well pleased" (Mt 3:17).

This occurred prior to the temptation of Jesus by the devil, and prior to his first miracle at Cana. It occurred before Jesus had begun his earthly ministry. What we can discern from biblical accounts is that Jesus grew up as a Jewish carpenter, helping his father Joseph in and around the village of Nazareth. We also know from biblical accounts that the young boy Jesus spent time in the synagogues, reading from the scrolls. These two factors (physical sturdiness and spiritual training), memorizing the Father's words and doing His will as a fleshly man (incarnate), greatly pleased the Father. If I were able to speak to every millennial young person today, I'd advise them to seek a vocation and study God's word in preparation to being "in the world, but not of the world" (Jn 17:16-18). They are not of this world as I am not of this world. As you sent me into the world, so I have sent them into the world. We need courage to enter this risky environment, and courage is not genetic – it is learned.

In a scene in the movie *Saving Private Ryan*, the Tom Hanks character is at a division headquarters enlisting a German-speaking young lad into his merry band of soldiers. The young lad wants to take his typewriter, a German helmet, and other items with him on the journey. But he attempts a feeble effort to say he is not qualified to be a foot soldier because the Army gave him a typewriter, not a rifle. The captain asks if he fired a weapon in basic training. The soldier affirms he did. The captain tells him to get his gear and the rifle and to get moving. No, the typewriter was not included in his gear, rather the captain held up a pencil instead and told him that would be his tool. Don't miss the teaching moment here! Yes, we are trained in a skill set, but when the application comes to us, we modify to fit the context. Also note he was allowed, even ordered, to bring the pencil and the rifle into battle. Plus, he was bilingual, and we all know what the mission was – to save another man.

David Livingstone, a nineteenth-century British hero and missionary, wrote in his journal concerning his courage. In Africa he was attacked by a lion, which he shot twice:

> It charged and caught me by the shoulder and we both came to the ground together. Growling horribly, he shook me as a terrier dog does a rat. Seeing several natives approaching to attack him, the lion sprung upon two of them, biting one in the thigh and the other in the shoulder. But at that moment the bullets the great beast had received took effect and he fell over dead.[6]

Livingstone had eleven tooth marks as permanent scars and the bone at the top of his left arm was crushed to splinters. The imperfect setting of this bone produced a stiff arm and caused much suffering the rest of his life. Yes indeed, much of ministry we do can have a serious effect on our bodies, and Jesus knows this. At the same time, it builds rapport with the locals and establishes relationship apart from theological doctrine.

BIVO is not contrary to biblical mandate or teaching. Below are some examples and applications from the Bible for bivocational activity:

Genesis 1:28 – Then God blessed them and said, "be fruitful and multiply." We are to be about the business and increase of God's Kingdom-in every way possible.

Numbers 14:24 – "But my servant Caleb has a different attitude than the others have. He has remained loyal to me, so I will bring him into the land he explored. His descendants will possess their full share of that land." Caleb represents the "pioneer spirit" even in old age and a willingness to be challenged with difficult jobs. His story also reminds the true believer that "retirement" is not in the cards. Our seniors especially need to be used mightily in the work of discipling and training the younger ones.

Judges 7: 4, 6 – "But the Lord told Gideon, 'There are still too many! Bring them down to the spring, and I will test them to determine who will go with you and who will not.' Only 300 of the men drank with their hands." This passage represents a good shepherd

PROVERBS 30: 19-19
B.F. H—

role; men and women who keep one eye out for feeding the sheep with the gospel message and another eye on dangers they may face while working in the same environment as the flock.

I Kings 19:19 – "So Elijah went and found Elisha son of Shaphat plowing a field. There were twelve teams of oxen in the field, and Elisha was plowing the twelfth team. Elijah went over to him and threw his cloak across his shoulders and then walked away." I love this example. The Older Prophet seeks a disciple to train and the Spirit leads him to a field where we encounter amazing skill on display. A typical good driver of Oxen handles two pairs comfortably, and Elisha is working with twelve! Jesus chose blue-collar disciples who like himself learned a trade before entering the ministry.

I Cor 9:3-7 – "Or is it only I and Barnabas who lack the right to not work for a living? Who serves as a soldier at his own expense? Who plants a vineyard and does not eat its grapes? Who tends a flock and does not drink the milk?" The BIVO example here is how Paul traveled with Barnabas and Timothy, and set a classic example of discipleship. During this time, Paul worked with his hands and gave credit to others who did the same. Men and women in the "Way" followed his BIVO example who did not come from the class of Pharisees or Sadducees. They will be called the lay leaders.

I Cor 9:19-23 – "I have become all things to all people so that by all possible means I might save some. I do all this for the sake of the gospel, that I may share in its blessings." Identity in Christ is a beautiful thing. This passage encourages us to believe the value in unique giftedness of all people to proclaim the gospel in the marketplace.

Rev 3:16 – "But since you are like lukewarm water, neither hot nor cold, I will spit you out of my mouth!" We cannot fall into the trap of being simply "takers and not doers" of the word. We are designed to be servants and to edify, teach, build each other up, and to love "holistically."

THE HAMMER

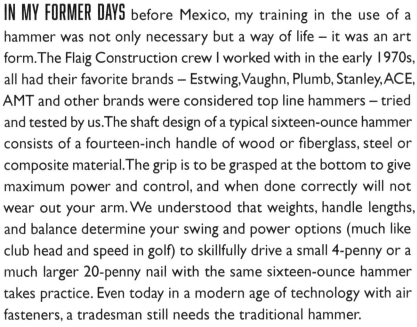

IN MY FORMER DAYS before Mexico, my training in the use of a hammer was not only necessary but a way of life – it was an art form. The Flaig Construction crew I worked with in the early 1970s, all had their favorite brands – Estwing, Vaughn, Plumb, Stanley, ACE, AMT and other brands were considered top line hammers – tried and tested by us. The shaft design of a typical sixteen-ounce hammer consists of a fourteen-inch handle of wood or fiberglass, steel or composite material. The grip is to be grasped at the bottom to give maximum power and control, and when done correctly will not wear out your arm. We understood that weights, handle lengths, and balance determine your swing and power options (much like club head and speed in golf) to skillfully drive a small 4-penny or a much larger 20-penny nail with the same sixteen-ounce hammer takes practice. Even today in a modern age of technology with air fasteners, a tradesman still needs the traditional hammer.

The head shape with a curved claw is five inches from tip of the claw to the face of the head, for use in laying shingles on a roof. Yes, the spacing of a shingle is five inches, and without technology the skill learned is nearly as fast as today's pneumatic guns. A modification for the roofing hammer involves a square head with waffle groves and a weight of twenty-two ounces. It sports a screw knob that can be set at five, five-and-a-half, six, or six-and-a-half inches for shingle spacing. The AJC hammer comes with a razor on the back side, replacing the curved claw feature. This serves the tradesman well because it can cut and slice the asphalt shingle easily and allows for speed, instead of the typical utility knife needed for cutting. To this day I use an Estwing sixteen-ounce for most projects and occasionally a twenty-two ounce for demo work. Obviously, these were the days before pneumatic air nail guns were used.

My father-in-law Milt used a Plumb brand sixteen-ounce curved claw, and not until he was well into his sixties could I beat him in a nail race. I became one of the fastest nailers on our crew, able to hold and finger a fist full of nails and strike like a machine repeatedly for hours. It became a skill set I learned well, turning the head of the nail and placing it in the way of the hammer in motion. Sledgehammers or mauls, sometimes called single or double jacks, range in weight from four to twelve pounds and are useful in setting joists, plywood, and walls into position. The key elements of the swing include balance, rhythm, and posture.

But I laid down my hammers to become a missionary in Mexico, including time at the REY Church with five young elders in their mid-twenties. These were men who became the core leader group and each one of them grew up without a father figure in their lives. They were mostly larger, heavier men than me, strong as bulls but

inexperienced in matters of vocational trade work. As an Apostolic Missionary Church Planter, my role was to teach these young men how to bust a hole in a concrete block wall with a ten-pound sledgehammer. The project underway was to create a water purification plant inside their REY Church building, and we needed a ten-foot square hole in the exterior wall. Having marked out the area, I took the first few swings and created a small hole. We passed the sledge back and forth for a little while between the men, and soon they realized the blows that had the most effect on the wall-were coming from me-not them. They were frustrated and curious as to how I struck the wall with authority and they could not.

I taught them these simple principles of the hammer: First, allow the head of the hammer to do the work, not your shoulder or power in your arms. The weight and shape of the head is sufficient to produce a power strike needed to make a dent. Second, aim your strike to a weak point in the wall, keeping in mind the shape of the block and that it has hollow areas and is not solid in the middle, only on the edges. Third, stop choking up on the handle – grab hold of the end of the wooden handle like the end of a baseball bat. Only when a batter needs to bunt will he choke up toward the barrel of the bat. Fourth, place your feet in a spread formation at a ninety-degree angle from the wall, about three feet apart and three feet from the wall (think Javelin-throwing posture). Fifth, allow your swing to begin from your hip and make sure your legs are involved with the swing move until the hammer and your shoulders have come around to face the wall. The blow will terminate with you facing the wall, but your two feet are one behind the other, similar to a golf driver on a tee-off or the way a golfer strikes the ball from beside and behind a little.

They caught on quickly. It wasn't long before we had a big pile of rubble to clean up. I developed personal relationships with each one of them, went to their colleges, homes, and places of work often just to be with them. I paid specific attention to Jose Nolasco, the Pastor of the REY Church and placed my efforts toward developing him as a theologian and a good shepherd of the flock. Today, Jose is one of the solid young leaders in the FIEL church, who also works closely with the "Old Guard" EFCA in Mexico. His model of Church is one of Holistic ministry, turning his church into a community center for immigrants in Mexico City, and the water plant is thriving, too. One of the leaders of the FIEL church is Dionisio, who is BIVO in practice. He owns an aluminum window and door shop and has employees from the church he pastors. I felt blessed because on a personal note, they never once called me a "gringo."

I think it is because I was willing to do life with them – OIKOS. More on the water plants later.

A footnote about Dionisio: He is a man of means and in good standing in his mountain community and amongst the brothers in Christ. A few years ago, he had lots of help building a new aluminum shop front, home, and church below. The structure was on the side of a steep cliff, and as you drive past the frontage area in the village, his aluminum shop is at the middle level or street level. It is his bivocational ministry you notice first, which he uses to provide work for the locals and service to surrounding community. Some questioned having the aluminum frame business store front as the center piece, as opposed to the church. Why was the church area below and not at street level? He was criticized, and the project was deemed "non-reproducible" by mission heads at the time. I also was not fully understanding the priority of placing the shop at street level, until it dawned on me how it was his personal ministry and holistic footprint. See Luke 8:1-3 about how women supported Jesus through their own means and laborers and workers.

Today, I'd tell you how what I saw and witnessed by the teams and laborers over the few years to help build this structure in Tlanchinol, Mexico was a very good investment. Why? Because a tool was given, a man's worth was improved so he could in turn be of great benefit to others when the tithe was insufficient for specific ministry needs. He not only employed villagers, he preached the gospel on Sunday and every day in-between in the marketplace environment. He gained respect, and to this day has used the gift of a structure to multiply God's kingdom. Besides all of this, if you understand trade work at all, there needs to be ease of access, sensible storage of material, consideration for a customer who can walk in easily and chose a style of track or edging. Market forces are at play here, and common sense for parking vehicles off the street during closing hours. By the way, the view from the church veranda below was not inhibited by anything. It was a fantastic view from the sanctuary, of the valley below, pure and natural.

Ecclesiastes 2:24 talks about how a man can nothing better than to eat and drink and find satisfaction in his work. This too, I see is from the hand of God, for without Him, who can eat or find enjoyment?

CALLED TO BE SERVANTS

ACCORDING TO THE GRACE of God given to me, like a skilled master builder I laid a foundation, and someone else is building upon it. Let each one take care how he builds upon it (1 Corinthians 3:10).

What BIVO Is

BIVO is a method of developing and equipping the saint/servant by investing time, finances and training in the marketplace. I believe there can be other types of BIVO, but this particular model includes teaching and training, and then releasing the novice into work and ministry.

> *It is for the called, to reach people for Jesus, and it is reproducible*

The Called are called to be servants just as Christ served, and we are to follow in His footsteps. These footsteps took Jesus to various places around the country and region, andtook the disciples and followers of Jesus to the ends of the earth as well. We are called to be subject to our masters (plural context), both the good ones and the unjust ones. It is clear (1 Pt 2:18,19) that this includes our boss, clients, or anyone in the marketplace who has a contractual agreement with you. "For it is a gracious thing, when mindful of God, one endures sorrows while suffering unjustly." Verse 20b: "But if when you do good and suffer for it you endure, this is a gracious thing in the sight of God." You want to grow, don't you? Then be doers of the Word! We are called to face trials of all kinds for testing our faith (Jas 1:2). Romans 10:14-15 teaches us we are called to testify, preach and teach in places apart from the church building.

In the profession as a tradesman, we receive an enormous amount of criticism (some justified) for either the work we do or the work we don't do. It can cost us a great deal of time, finances and effort to do what we say we are going to do. Some don't even show up in a timely manner or they put the client on hold for a long time. The point is, if a bivocational pastor is going to make a commitment to discipling someone, it is understood there will be costs, personal and otherwise. I have learned that the best investment you can make in life is in another person.

Called to reach people for Jesus: We are sent to be ministers of reconciliation, to be faithful servants to our masters in the marketplace. Acts 9:40-43 – After Peter raised a woman from the dead, "…he stayed in Joppa for many days with one Simon, a tanner." The Gospel of Christ and the formation of the "WAY" grew exponentially here in the marketplace.

When my wife and I arrived in Mexico City in 2006, we had a box of Christian tracts (*Quien es Jesus*) given to us by an individual supporter. In the "second largest city" in the world there is major influence brought to bear in the rest of Latin America. This international city is chalk full of mom and pop businesses, people who have influence and standing. We knew it was also ripe with unbelievers, and our message was important to the workers. The box of 3,000 tracts was empty when we left in 2014, mostly given out one by one. We will not know the full value of this effort on this side of heaven. But we can read and understand that Joppa was a city of influence and it served the cause well, to exponentially advance the gospel.

Reproducible: Because this is God's plan. It works and there is no plan B (Jas 2:14-17). Faith without works is dead. In the early days of the Way in Acts 2, when the believers shared possessions, do you think the sale of land they possessed to fund ministry was sufficient to carry on indefinitely? No. Although it is honorable to share our possessions, it also an honor to work for a living. This model is reproducible because faith is active with a bivocational pastor and with his work his faith then is completed (Jas2: 22). I Peter2:17 says to honor everyone. Love the brotherhood. Fear God. Honor the Emperor.

Evangelism outside of the Box by Rick Richardson[7] points to new ways to help people experience the good news. People are looking for communities in which faith is lived out and spiritual experiences are tangible. How do we do the work of creating a compelling moral and spiritual vision in our day? We imitate the Apostle Paul in using the culture and its forms to reach people.

AND GOD MADE IT GROW   I COR. 3 VS 5-10

A later chapter of this book is about transformation and how it becomes a new identity in a believer's life. The revelation of Jesus in the bible teaches we will someday have new names written on white stones. I believe these new names will be because of our ministry in Christ at whatever capacity in His kingdom on earth.

David Gustafson on on EFCA History and BIVO[8]

"In America, bivocational pastors emerged out of necessity when new congregations did not have resources to support them. Even when churches had resources, some preferred bivocational ministry. For example, colonial ministers of the Church of England in the 1600s maintained themselves by means of the *parson's glebe*, a piece of land set aside for the pastor's use to support himself. Moreover, many Southern Baptist congregations were led by a farmer-preacher who tilled ground, split rails, planted corn, fed hogs, preached sermons, performed weddings and conducted funerals.

Furthermore, early Evangelical Free Church preachers in America were mostly bivocational. At the 1884 Boone Conference that was called to discuss theological questions regarding the nature and practice of the church, the 22 who attended were mostly itinerant evangelists and lay preachers who served one or more newly established congregations.

Twenty years later, however, one church after another was calling a resident pastor. This caused tension between two schools of thought: E. A. Halleen, former president of the Swedish Evangelical Free Church who went on to become the first president of the EFCA, favored resident pastors; August Davis, an early pastor in the Swedish Evangelical Free Church, preferred itinerant preachers who traveled for a few months of the year to minister to the congregations. During the rest of the year, the itinerant preachers earned a living from farming or their trade.

As local churches became more established, resident pastors became the common practice.

Throughout church history, God has led His people to carry out His mission in the world through pastors and missionaries who have supported themselves, as well as through those who were supported by churches. From the beginning, tentmaking missionaries like Paul's emerged, serving both voluntarily and by necessity. Where Christianity was established, and local churches received adequate funding—generally in cities—fully funded pastors became the norm.

Today, however, as the West becomes increasingly post-Christian, bivocational ministry is again a viable means to proclaim the gospel, offering it free of charge (1 Corinthians 9:18). It may be time to rethink the 'professional ministry model' of Christendom and again consider the validity of bivocational ministry. It has not merely a biblical basis but a long history."

A FIRST CHOICE

Intentional Strategy and Multiplication (Train-Equip-Release)

A FIRST-CHOICE TACTIC: OUR problems of church growth and lack of training cannot be solved using the same thinking that created them (modifying a famous Albert Einstein quote). Good tactics can save even the worst strategy. Bad tactics will destroy even the best strategy. When Jesus instructed the disciples to cast the net on the other side, it became a teachable lesson for them while working hard in the marketplace. While we are to be fishers of men, we do so where the men and women can be found apart from the inner  sanctuary of the church. One of the foundational concepts of the church include expanding the Kingdom (The Jabez Prayer, I Chron 4:10, which will be covered later in this book).

In *Total Church* by Tim Chester and Steve Timmis[9] they explain how the gospel is a missionary word, so the church must be missionary centered. We wrestle with making the gospel relevant to the world. But in this story, God is about the business of transforming the world to fit the shape of the gospel. The clear majority of Christians have not been helped to see that who they are and what they are and what they do every day in schools. workplaces or clubs is significant to God, nor that the people they spend time with in those everyday contexts are the people God is calling them to pray for bless and witness to. See Acts 10:34-35, and in *Total Church* see pages 19, 32, 35, 36, 45, and 79.

The Dunbar Tactic: John Dunbar is the main character in the film *Dances with Wolves.* What can we learn about strategy and tactics from his story? The strategy: A bivocational pastor places himself or herself into a unique culture setting to gain understanding. Likewise, John Dunbar placed himself into a culture to be able to learn firsthand a unique culture. Second, he learned the language and adapted his lifestyle to the people of the culture without compromising that culture or his own uniqueness. Third, with honor and respect he assimilated into the target culture as one of them but still different. Lastly, and perhaps sadly, the government interrupted the ambiance created by Dunbar and critically injured the possibility of understanding this culture (Deut. 25:4 "You shall not muzzle the Ox when it is treading out the grain"). Since believers are ambassadors for Christ, and some go places the church body does not go, then let us support them, recognizing special skills and calling with certain believers.

The beautiful feet strategy (Ro 10:14-17): How will people know about God or grow spiritually if they don't attend a church regularly? Again, not to diminish or negate the congregational experience, but rather to demonstrate the love of the church, a BIVO pastor represents the good shepherd seeking his sheep. Sometimes all that is required for a man and his family to re-enter into fellowship with the body is simply to be invited and to be valued. And when we encounter either believers or non-believers, our first action should be to value them by striking up a conversation because they don't care what you know until they know you care.

Gary Thomas in *Authentic Faith*[10] says it this way: "Wherever you go whether it's the golf course, a church conference room, a restaurant or the local mall we have opportunity to open up our eyes to what is happening to others around us, to think thoughts bigger than those that concern only us, and to be used by God-if only just by noticing others-by caring, in large ways and small and by getting involved." And "If you truly want to experience an authentic faith, go where people are hurting the most and get involved in their lives. You'll not only see God at work, you'll also gain his heart and very likely become transformed in the process."

Testing Ground: 2 Timothy 2:15 A worker Approved by God

When Jesus approaches a person for ministry duty, he is able recognize their character and if the person is going to be receptive and open to learning.

Walking on the Matanuska Glacier near Sutton, Alaska, we stepped into a silt – mud, refined and creamy, ready for molding on a potter's wheel. The artisans come to gather it up and form pottery. It also turns a different color while being fired in the kiln from a gray to an orange and white color. Recognizing character – the illustration is simply: this type of precipitated mud is already useful for forming, and capable of withstanding high heat in the kiln without being destroyed.

THE HAMMER & THE PULPIT

The illustration and application here are that the Holy Spirit changes a person, but there is a due-diligence process others do to help form character.

Ananias Acts chapter 9 was directed to go and find a man named Saul and lay hands on him. He knew the reputation of Saul and at first wanted nothing to do with him, but the Lord directed him to Saul. After laying hands on the blinded Saul, he became Paul and now could see, and he grew strong in the Lord, in part because of the disciple Ananias. There was to be a specific purpose to Paul's ministry, bringing the gospel to the gentiles. We know that for such a time as this, God uses specific men and women to be a voice and a testament to Him.

I remember in Sunday School once, it was noted that a man with Paul's background and resumé would cause many church boards today to reject him. After all, he was a persecutor, caused riots, was a Roman Citizen, spent time in jail, was shipwrecked, snake-bitten, and on and on. But what if God needs men and women who, like Paul, are part of the un-loved or un-lovely types? What if the precipitate process works on those who are ready for a life of ministry? The old saying, "you can't teach an old dog a new trick" is for dogs, not humans. The men who were fishing when Jesus approached had some theological training but did not make muster to become a Pharisee or a Sadducee. They knew how to work hard, and probably experienced failure in their lives as well as success along the way. But they were ready to follow Jesus. The second they committed to learning something new they were involved personally in the precipitate process, ready to be refined like diamonds in the rough.

A firm foundation requires a compaction process which pre- pares the ground for the rest of the work, which translates into ROCK SOLID CHRISTIANS. The Testing ground is a person, not a place, who has committed themselves to a process of disciple- ship (through a saving faith in Jesus), which comes with spiritual benefits as well as financial. The concept of on-the-job training is not a new one, but training a layperson to be self-sufficient and capable of supporting their ministry is the BIVO strategy to reach the lost. After having been proved by the rigors of the physical and mental tasks, a lay person applies the knowledge of the skill set which produces wisdom. Once the precipitate process has been accomplished, some laymen will advance to more mature and difficult matters. The refinement of Gold process is God's idea (Mt 7:24-27). Build the house on a rock-solid foundation that will not fall so the building that comes next won't fall either.

Oneness Embraced by Tony Evans[11] engages in a conversation about Petra, a theological discussion of Rocks. Jesus used the Greek word Petra indicative of a mass or cliff of rocks that is comprised of something much larger than any individual rock. This mass of rocks interlinks individual rocks together to create a stronger whole. While there are a multitude of rocks in Petra, they do not function as individual rocks, but are intimately joined together (see 1 Peter 2:5). The Church is therefore uniquely positioned and authorized to carry out the mandates of the Kingdom under the authority of Christ, when we seek the Kingdom above all else (Eph 1:22, 23).

We are from the ground, soil and rock, and the life of a true Christian can be marked with one sifting process after another. It is a constant daily struggle against Satan, self, and society. But God desires to put us through this consolidation or testing process as He prepares us to be "fitly framed" into His Holy Temple, as mentioned in Ephesians 2:21. So as we consider dirt, clay, and rocks the point is this: In precious metal operations ore is the chief source of gold. God chose each of us "in the raw" like an unrefined chunk of ore (1 Cor 1:26-28). God calls the weak, base, foolish and despised of the earth. We ourselves were not the finest of ore when God first selected us.

Isaiah 64:8 – "We are the clay and you are our Potter; we are the work of your hand." Romans 9:21 – "Has the potter no right over the clay, to make out of the same lump one vessel for honorable use and another for dishonorable use?"

You must beat and pound the air out of a lump of clay before it can even go to a wheel or under the knife or goad. It is like a precipitate process where the clay is thrown down hard, suddenly, to expunge the air inside. If any air exists yet inside a lump, then it will explode in the heating process inside the kiln. If the ground is not compacted correctly with pressure and water, it will not hold the building process that is coming (Luke 6:48). Likewise, if an individual is not properly vetted or purified for higher-level ministry, they will fail under the pressure. The pottery then becomes useful for limited projects, and in some cases dishonorable use or ignoble uses. You can park a heavy truck on ground that is ninety percent shale, but do not attempt to build a house on this type of soil.

This testing is not the same as Sanctification process. In my view, the selection of the raw material in the form of people who can learn and can be malleable need to be tested to determine the next step in their spiritual journey. The sanctification process is beyond the compaction process and then continues through a believer's life until death.

Milton Flaig in Nevada #13

VISION

WHY PRACTICE? IN A "blue collar illustration," Jesus demonstrated to the disciples "where to cast the net" to catch fish, and by a "blue collar application" revealed to them how they will be fishers of men. We practice bivocational ministry because this strategy works to expand the kingdom. Not that God cannot be found in the Church, rather it's that God is always seeking, always entering our lives, always looking for his lost sheep. Part of the important response to Christian living is to congregate with other believers and grow in maturity, just as steel sharpens steel.

The Industrial Revolution is the name given the movement in which machines changed people's way of life. It began in Britain in the late 1700s. Manufacturing was often done in people's homes, using hand tools or basic machines. Industrialization marked a shift to powered, special-purpose machinery, factories, and mass production. In today's world, a modern-day movement with roots to "The Way" (Is 30:21; Mt 5:16; Acts 9:2) is aptly named BIVO that once again calls out to men and women to walk in a missionary manner and let our light shine before others. This is a modern day "game-changer" and underscores an old saying: "A man who chops his own fire wood warms himself twice," meaning there is great benefit to nurturing the DNA characteristic of OIKOS by being real in a community. The shift to powered, special-purpose machinery, factories, and mass production indicates a reproduceable model. So, a Spirit-powered novice, with a special purpose, who is equipped and ready for ministry, will produce fruit and multiply. The factories then become training centers or community centers that meet specific needs for the marginalized. These centers can be supported by the local churches and suddenly we have mass production with the church equipped to stand in the gap. Front line ministry at its best!

NO Work or profit in Sheol. Ecclesiastes 9:9-10 – "Enjoy life with the wife whom you love, all the days of your vain life that he has given you under the sun, because that is your portion in life and in your toil at which you toil under the sun. Whatever your hand finds to do, do it with all your might, for there is no work or thought or knowledge or wisdom in Sheol, to which you are going." Revelation 18 reveals a world market system that will fall to judgement by God. Jesus commanded us to make disciples of all nations, which makes the world market system prime territory. Hell will

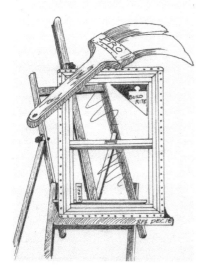

be full of people who did it their way and who were greedy on earth. But they won't have a chance to work off their mistakes, so while there is still time, we preach Christ and we work by the sweat of our brow.

Jobs are created when knowledge spreads. BIVO is a balance of Holistic/Spiritual mix, with on-the-job training ministry. It is like an "Externship" (similar to an internship) where rapid growth is expected. The trainee now has a new job and can be refined during the training and almost immediately apply his skill set to earn a living as a self-employed pastor. If I train a prospective young artist to use a brush with both left and right hands when painting window frames, don't you see how he can use this skill to earn a living? I do, and know so. Regardless of modern tech gear, a gifted skilled painter is still a needed entity in the right context.

3000 Windows: In 1980s Rapid City, South Dakota, commercial painting became one of the arrows of experience in my quiver. I was trained by professional painters in states like Nevada and South Dakota, becoming very adept at floating-taping-sanding, texture-vinyl wall coverings, spray painting, and brush and roll. But the skill of holding a brush in either hand and becoming accurate and fast soon became my trademark. This may appear to be a "sidetrack," but let me assure you that every move with the brush is critical. Dipping a two-and-a-half-inch angle sash into the paint so that a third of the brush has paint, then touching both sides quickly but gently, is key to bringing the product up to meet the work surface. The type of brush is critical for trim painting. If it is too small it will require many more moves to the supply bucket, and if it is too large it becomes a club and is cumbersome. This simple step keeps the paint from dripping all over, and makes the brush properly loaded for service. I Timothy 3:7 – "Moreover, he must be well thought of by outsiders, so that he may not fall into disgrace, into a snare of the devil."

If I am "cutting in" on the left of a glass, then I use my left hand, and if on the right side of the glass I use the right hand. This trick allows the correct angle of the brush in relation to the surface being painted.It also develops speed and accuracy. The term "cutting in" means a sharp line is drawn to terminate a body of paint, such as in the corner of a wall or around a doorknob or with multi-pane glass windows. This term is just what it sounds like in carpentry – when you measure and cut/saw or knife to fit a piece. "Cutting in" or "knife in" or "trimming a straight edge" is something that can be taught and requires repetition to become a master. This will eliminate a lot of masking on a painting project and helps glean a decent profit by saving time from all the masking many people do.

Another important skill set involved with painting is proper brush care and cleaning. Your brush needs to be kept in a condition that will assure a sharp cutting edge, and this requires using a steel brush to remove dry paint and a pressure of water down into the heel to remove any paint below the bristle line. From a spiritual perspective, I would teach the novice a life lesson or have a teachable moment by saying "Keep your edge by staying clean and unsoiled from the world, and by filling your mind with the words in the Bible," as is mentioned in James 2.

By the time West Hills Painting won the contract with Skull Construction for the Ellsworth Airbase project, I was already a master painter. The job called for replacing 3000 windows and re-siding the barracks on the Air Base. Pella Window Corp won the bid to supply the raw wood windows straight from the factory in Iowa. But every one of them needed to be advanced to eighty percent painted prior to installation. The double-hung windows came in one/two/three mulled sections and were delivered to a warehouse on Deadwood Avenue during the winter months from January to March. We used space heaters and massive tarps to create a warm painting booth. Each window needed to be stripped of all hardware and primed, then second-coated, and then re-packaged for delivery to the Air base. I proved to be one of the fastest painters on our team, able to complete 21 first-coated windows an hour. Only one other man was as fast – Irv Holland, and he was a master before I was hired by West Hills Painting. Another key step to prepping the window is the sanding and calking of fine line cracks and roughness of the wood. With a damp cloth, 220-grit sandpaper and a calking gun, each unit was groomed and dusted with an old dry brush prior to applying the paint. So this became another trade mark of mine – doing extensive prep-work before touching the brush to any surface – and this too is a professional skill that can be taught.

The spiritual application: Do your research about a subject in scripture to discover the correct context before making a life application example for today's world.

Have you ever heard how the Chinese use two brush strokes to write the word *crisis*? One brush stroke stands for danger; the other for opportunity. In a crisis, beware of danger – but recognize the opportunity. While some Mandarin linguistics specialists don't refer to these two strokes together as a literal meaning, for purposes of my illustration with learning to use a brush, it produced opportunity for me. I have been in a mini crisis whenever I was without work and needed to earn a living. The skill sets we can teach and pass on to others will produce opportunity with options to earn a living rather than receiving a hand-out when it presents itself.

How does this tie into bivocational ministry? For one thing, I had begun to do side projects for pastors and missionaries, offering my services free of charge. The more chances I got to spread my wings, the closer I came to starting my own construction company.

I soon discovered, however, that putting my skills to use on "side work" made for bad relations with my boss. One day on a weekend he followed me to a project of mine and fired me from West Hills painting. He said, "If you think you are ready to go on your own, then [expletives] you can start paying taxes like I do and be a bona fide contractor. It hurt at first, but it was the best thing that ever happened in my trade career. Proverbs 19:8 – The one who gets wisdom loves life: the one who cherishes understanding will soon prosper. Shortly after I was fired, there was an ad in the paper, similar to Angie's list, where an apartment complex was seeking bids to re-paint their exterior windows. They had on average three main widows (a single 3X5, a double 5X6 and a triple 5X9 pane) per apartment, and there were twenty-four units. I bid on seventy-five windows and twenty-four doors and finished the project in one week, with one coat of primer and two coats of the finish color because I was so fast! Best money I ever made, and it more than paid the bills and met my average monthly take home earnings. I had discovered during my training period that I was ambidextrous and able to paint efficiently with either hand.

A theologian once said, "Don't ever get tired of taking people back to the Bible." I say, "Don't stray from the basic skill sets you learn when facing change." These learned skill sets represent what "metanoia is for spiritual application" is to skill set training for surviving in a feast or famine workplace environment.

In Denver, at a BIVO seminar, I met Hugh Halter and was not surprised to see his choice of house painting as a base model for BIVO. In fact, some of the wealthiest contractors in the world are painting contractors. Educated people can demand higher pay rates. The science involved with knowing thinners, solvents, and glues requires top notch learning ability. Basic skill sets can be used (holding a brush correctly, loading the paint brush with product, training to use both hands to paint with accuracy and cleanliness, and cleaning the brush), but there is so much more to teach. Where there is a talent for plastering, tape and texture, or various stucco type finishes, it can be developed and refined. Spray rigs/pots/machines come in all sizes, and skills in these areas need to be addressed. How do you install vinyl in commercial buildings? What types of finishes work best with antique building trims? What is the difference between finishes such as egg shell, matte, or flat, and where do they belong? How do you apply paint to exterior surfaces in hot humid climates, or cold dry areas? What are safe scaffolding systems, ladders placement techniques, and masking applications? Again, the idea is to discover what strengths a student has, and in what areas.

The DAYA Girls

Years before we even considered overseas mission work, Karla and I owned a craft business and supplemented our income with carpentry work on the side. Karla became a premium artist on our circuit. Her tole painting was well-known around the mid-west region, Montana, Colorado, South Dakota and Nebraska, even as far north as Idaho. She and I stayed busy producing up to 300 different product items for outlet shops in all these states, and also sold at special event shows for a company called Bear Crossing. We incorporated our family, and our church family, over the years in production of these crafts. Not surprisingly, when we became missionaries in Mexico City and subsequently she was introduced to an orphanage in the Cuajimalpa borough or municipality, she was very interested in working here. DAYA is a name given to the orphanage using two words in Spanish: Da is the command to "give" while the single "A" stands for amor (love), and a "y" in Spanish means "and." Forus, DAYA means "Give Love." It is a place that gives an opportunity for marginalized young girls without education and who are mothers raising babies. We were introduced to thirteen-year-old girls with wto-year-old babies, some with more than one child. The foundation is home for the girls until they reach the age of twenty-one. Some leave before then for various reasons. including an unwillingness to cope with rules.

The method of regeneration and education was simple at DAYA: Teach them responsibility for raising and caring for their babies, give them a chance at the equivalent of a GED high school certificate, in some cases get a birth certificate, and demonstrate the love of Jesus to them by teaching them a skill set or craft. Some were good at sewing, some at cooking, some were good artists, some were good at math or computer skills, some demonstrated good market and business savvy – all were street smart and under-  stood well words like harsh, dark, danger, hunger, rejection, and being marginalized by pimping aunts, uncles, and even parents. They needed hope.

Enter my wife I into their world – a match made in heaven! She likes to say, "I raised boys not girls," so getting a chance to become a mentor with up to twenty-four young ladies was a supreme honor and challenge for her. While I was occupied with mentoring two different church plants, she would travel to the DAYA house by public transportation with a back pack and spend time with the girls twice a week. By the time we moved to an area closer to the orphanage, the Desierto de Los Leones home, I was engaging with her on a more regular basis. Together on certain days we taught an art class, and the girls loved the special attention to their creative works. Making a piece of art is a form of expression that brings out their soul, their character and mind set. In many cases we saw giftedness and skill sets which could excel a girl into a vocation. DAYA used their funding campaigns to set up commercial kitchens, develop a preschool for the babies of the girls, and even included community children. This became a money-raising opportunity as well as their collection of donated items like a salvation army depot. The girls would help organize items from clothes to furniture and at the same time learn how to be a contributor in the entire foundation. They would set up the weekly market day and help collect the revenue. In the story of Ruth 1:16 she said, "Your people will be my people and your God will be my God." And when Naomi and Ruth arrived in Bethlehem at the beginning of the barley harvest, they went to the property of Boaz to glean the fields. The DAYA girls are like a modern-day Ruth, each one of them.

As the needs presented themselves, both Karla and I ministered for nearly six years here at the DAYA house, which included a remodel of the current facility for the preschool. I became the handyman for the compound, repairing roofs, doors, painting walls, building beds, fixing plumbing and whatever building needs came up. At one point we called in short-term teams to move along the remodel of the school. Eventually it opened and soon was filled with other children from the local community as well as with DAYA children. Karla and I became like parents to the girls. We shared our home with them and got to know the uniqueness of each of them. And one day it became clear our mission to Mexico City was closing. It was time to move the girls along in their spiritual development, even though most of them claimed to be from Catholic families, others had exposure to the dark side with Santo-Muerto or the Saint of Death.

We needed to find a safe church for the girls, a place they would feel comfortable attending. They needed to cement their growing relationship with Jesus and to be baptized. In fact, this was our final strategy as the days in Mexico were ending for us. We used to take the girls to church by walking hand-in-hand eight block away, sometimes with more than twenty of them. I remember the first day we took them to the Fraternidad Church with pastor Arizmendi. We arrived a bit late and filed in to fill three rows of chairs, sort of disrupting the opening part of the service. To their surprise, a group of ladies approached them and handed them tambourines as the worship music began. The girls soon had favorite songs they would sing even at DAYA away from the church during the week. The day came for a group of girls to go and interview with church elders about being baptized. This was a nervous point for Karla and I, because now each girl would be giving a reason for their own personal faith and explain what they knew about Jesus. Our work proved out through the interviews and several girls were baptized, praise the Lord! This is a condensed version of the story of DAYA, and perhaps more about this ministry will be written in another book about our ten years in Mexico. But consider this: What would you expect to be a fitting conclusion to a ministry you have invested in? I Corinthians 2:9 – "No eye has seen; no ear has imagined what God has prepared for those who love him." In our case, the fitting end of our time with the girls was to see and experience their baptism, a public confession of faith based on an internal state of new life and new hope inside them.

One last comment on this encounter with God's creation: We considered the important action of giving up our life as we knew it in America. We pushed our chips to the center of the table, gave up our working role, and assumed a humble posture of following Jesus so he could make us fishers of men. What we were willing to give up, the Lord gave right back again into our hands: The opportunity to demonstrate the hands and feet of Jesus to needy young women. We absolutely trust Jesus to open doors of opportunity, and He will for you as well. All you need to do is to say yes to his leading. This is HIS plan for salvation.

IDEA

THE CONTEXT OF AN environment gives clues and even road maps to enter into a specific community with a gospel message. Ask yourself, who gets to flourish or benefit because of your service? God designed us for service and stewardship, to thrive and prosper. Just like a palette of paint presents choices for the artist, so does the unique individual present complex and multiple options for presenting the gospel or teaching a skill set. Proverbs 5:1 – "Drink water from your own cistern, flowing water from your own well."

One of the major Universities in Mexico City, ITN (Institute Technical National) in the borough or municipality called Azcapotzalco became a ministry location for me teaching ESL (English as a second language). Campus Crusade could not get onto the campus because of their reputation for proselytizing and evangelizing. However, I could enter with my student badge as an alumnus of UNAM (University of Mexico-CEPE Program) and I began a recon mission in the library at ITN as motive and reason to operate legally on the campus. I discovered a textbook used by ITN called *Pensamiento Creativo*[12] (Creative Thinking). The authors (Ramón Longoria Ramírez, Irma Laura Cantú Hinojosa, and José Daniel Ruiz Sepúlveda) produced this book for the University Autonomous New Leon. I bought a copy and began to read it. Here are a few excerpts:

"The only educated man is one who has learned to learn, the man who has done this correctly, could adapt to changes." This is similar to what other contemporary writers like Carl Rogers have noted: "He has come to realize that no knowledge is safe by itself and that he has understood that only the process of knowing how to seek this knowledge will give him security." I understand this may sound confusing here, but in the translation of Spanish to English we sometimes lose the correct grammar. My takeaway from this saying is that we cannot be an expert in a matter unless we have tested the theory, done the work, done an action with the new knowledge, and tested our ability with this new knowledge. And as well, the process of seeking the knowledge is just as important. In other words, how we learn something, the process of learning, is something to be taught and applied.

As an aside, it has been noted that in Japan when an engineer graduates from college, he has only one phase left before getting his certificate. He must enter the work force and do physical hard labor on the type of projects he will someday design. It makes all the difference in the world to use your knowledge on the field to gain wisdom to lead others. I have always believed that wisdom comes from learning how to properly use knowledge.

Here are a few more gems from *Pensamiento Creativo*: "God is the Creator-Believe that there is a supreme God-Learn what the significance of life is and our role on earth – Engage in the spirit of serv-anthood. Develop and advance through your work." And "Creativity is the will of the Creator for me. I am a creative channel of God-His divine plan includes my work – I will bloom through this creativity."

I did not expect to find a chapter on God in a textbook on the campus, featuring the search for knowledge and how we are created in God's image! I began using the Spanish phrases to teach English. Each Thursday morning, I supplemented this material for ESL with a book called *The Evolution of a Creationist* by Jobe Martin.[13] The students began reading about amazing creatures such as birds, beetles, giraffes, lizards and more that Jobe Martin wrote about. The students eventually introduced me to a professor who offered her classroom in case of rain or bad weather. Two of the students joined our Church Plant REY, and its external bible study groups.

What are needs of the people in a marketplace environment? When we send our laity into the world, they will discover poverty at many levels they otherwise might not have known about. A BIVO pastor can act! Where there is lack of knowledge, they can educate the poor. Where there is opposition by powerful people, they can work for social justice in the marketplace. Where there is personal sin, they evangelize and disciple the poor. Where there is lack of resources, BIVO gives resources. "Let your light shine before others that they may see your good works" (Mt 5:14-16), this paragraph was adapted from the book *When Helping Hurts* by Steve Corbett and Brian Fikkert.[14]

The Juan Santos Story: Camino de Vida

We have been working with Camino de Vida for the last 10 years, we currently have about 90 people in attendance. Our services start at 1:00 pm every Sunday and we also meet every Wednesday night for prayer meetings. Our congregation has people from several countries, and we enjoy the diversity and the opportunities that it brings. I also have a part time job with Tyson foods as a Chaplain which gives me the opportunity to meet people on a regular basis. My job is to provide pastoral care, counseling and visitation to our team members and their families. I spend time with new people on a regular basis and that has had a great impact in the work we do in our community. My wife took a job as a counselor at the Lexington, Nebraska high school a few months ago; she has 300-plus students in her workload and that has also provided many opportunities for us to minister not only to the student body but to their families as well. The Lord has opened many doors for us to work in Lexington; even though there've been times when we are about to quit; the Lord continues to give us the strength and to use us as a family for His glory and purposes. About three months ago we welcomed Juanita, a young lady from Guatemala, into our home. She came to the United States by herself about a year ago at the age of fourteen with the desire of getting an education to be able to help her mother in a small village in Guatemala. My wife met Juanita at the school and knew she did not have a home so she invited her to stay with us. We are praying for her and for God's direction for her life. Juanita enjoys coming to church with us and spending time with my sister who is visiting us from Mexico City. We are also thankful for our children

(Delilah, Andres and Esteban) and we are expecting baby number four. I also want to take the opportunity to share with you some prayer requests. We have been thinking about the possibility of bringing my brother David and his family from Mexico City to help with the ministry of Camino de Vida. He has been involved in several areas of ministry in Mexico for the last twenty years. He is a talented musician and his wife has experience working with women and children. We are praying for God's provision to be able to bring them to Lexington and for the process of obtaining the required visas as well. We want to thank the churches and individuals in the Midwest District for your prayers and financial support. I also want to recognize the work of Pastor Duane Russell and the Lexington EFC for their commitment to reaching out to the Hispanic community; we are thankful for what you do to advance the kingdom of God in Lexington.

Juan and Maria Santos

He who started the good work in you will carry it onto completion until the day of Christ Jesus.
Philippians 1:6

CRITICAL MASS

A CRITICAL MASS CAN be achieved by just one man and a student who practice innovation, invention and discovery. For example, Sir Richard Arkwright from England developed the spinning wheel.[15] The cotton manufacturers created a whole new class of people, "the urban proletariat." The structure of society itself would never be the same. The Proletariat class of the industrial age was the working class that provided manual labor. Roman culture recognized them as the lowest class in the culture. But God chose what is foolish in the world to shame the wise; God chose what is weak in the world to shame the strong; God chose what is low and despised in the world, even things that are not, to bring to nothing things that are (1 Cor 1:27-). Sir Arkwright applied his knowledge of the cotton industry to meet a growing need for production which resulted in even greater commerce, eventually affecting America. Critical mass can associate with the ground prep chatter, meaning at what point in a believer's life is he or she ready for action? Ready to apply training and skill like Gideon, who God used after he reduced the force down to the "critical mass" needed to accomplish the objective.

The Story of The Vasco De Quiroga

A smart move when entering unknown territory is to find someone who knows the terrain and culture. Arriving in Mexico City in 2006, we quickly realized we were babes in the woods, so to speak. We relied not only on our host family but also our missionary team, who for the first thirteen weeks in Mexico, were located sixty miles away from us. You then must listen to story, you notice patterns, you ask questions, and you observe the arts. At our first language school in Cuernavaca, the instructors used music and art plus strong conversational teaching methods to get us started in immersion Spanish. Each week we learned folk songs and experienced artisans of all types coming to the school and presenting their wares and telling stories. We soon realized that art forms such as pottery/ceramics and pottery clay products have distinct family lines and heritage. For example, Talevera Pottery is well known as some of the finest handmade pieces in Mexico. The same is true for items made from wool, such as the Poncho, horongo, or the paztquaro (a type of coat or covering used for cold, damp weather conditions). Something else we learned gradually was that certain regions of Mexico were known for specific artisan works. In Oaxaca they are known for their cheese, authentic dress style, and dancing. In other parts you discover silver mining, fine chocolate production, and of course coffee production.

For us, our early years in Mexico were drawing us further west into the city and into an area called Alvaro Obregon and the Cuajimalpa boroughs or municipalities. It was there in a barrio called Santa Fe (about the size of Denver, Colorado) that I discovered the Vasco de Quiroga. They say the streets in Mexico are typically named after bad men who ruled with viciousness and an iron hand. But one of the longest streets that winds thru this very modern Wall Street-looking area of Mexico City is called Vasco De Quiroga.

Vasco de Quiroga

So, I asked, "Who is this man and why does he have a street named after him?"

He was a monk, a priest in fact, and one of the first sent from Rome to help settle the indigenous groups outside of Mexico City.[16] He discovered a poverty of education, a poverty of resources to earn an income, and a poverty of relationship with God. Vasco began teaching from the Old Testament, but he taught them how to harness the local resources to earn an income. He taught them how to build looms and weave wool, how to produce copper and forge all sorts of useful items, and how to carve wood and care for themselves by giving them medical education. He eventually helped start the first hospital and then a second one in this area of the city. His statue is seen in the square in Santa Rosa Xochiac, not far from the National Forest called Desierto de Leones.

A famous bandito, Emilio Zapata (who is quoted as saying, "Men who work the ground are entitled to benefit from it and rule over it") resided in this area with his men because of its natural resources, namely the common village people and their skill sets. So, Vasco felt it necessary to teach Scripture and Capitalism at the same time. Why should we be any different today? Another chapter in this

book tells the story of the water purification plants I help start in two church plants here. It was a direct result of the study of the culture and who went before us years ago on this mission field. Vasco was bivocational. Today the state of Michoacán and parts of Toluca, Mexico City and surrounding area are known as some of the finest artisans in Latin America, in part because of the innovation and heart of one man. Something else I noticed: How wise was it for a pope or king (representing the CEO type, president of a company, or leadership at the top) to send a man from Rome who knew trade work intimately? Strategy starts at the top, which is why I refer to bivocational ministry as a *First-Choice* method of reaching the lost and marginalized.

ADJUSTS TO CHANGE

PER THE LATEST DATA (www.churchleadership.org), around 40% of Americans attend church regularly today. When we have roughly 60% of Christians appearing to be inactive, and there is clearly a disconnect and downward trend since 2008. The lowest percentage of believers not attending church falls into the ranks of the younger generations. Additionally, only one in ten Christians say Christ is the only way to eternal life. However, on a positive note, a billion people attend a small church in our world today. But the traditional church in America is facing another issue: The political pressure is increasingly giving rise to the possibility of the local church losing its tax-exempt status.

BIVO Presents the Future Track Now

- Provides opportunity where it does not currently exist.

- Trains and equips the whole person with a holistic ministry approach.

- Submits to growing keener in compliance with God's will.

- Can be a growth-producing treatment with changing demographics.

- Adapts to the changing context which is vital to church planting strategy.

- With 4,000-7,000 churches per year closing their doors, BIVO presents and opportunity to draw God's people back into fellowship.

THE HAMMER & THE PULPIT

- Is a teaching program of the Church/Christian worldview, a systematic training and demonstration of what we say about our ethical and work views with the various vocations of the saints.

- Brings back into play the term *technologia* or the study of art or skill within the body of believers. The Mexican Priest Vasco de Quiroga taught arts and crafts along with Old Testament teaching/training.

VALUES

Life on Life: From 1968 to 2006 I worked as a carpenter, beginning as a helper/laborer/apprentice and graduating to master/ journeyman/contractor/superintendent through a "Life on Life" method. I learned all kinds of skills by working alongside master teachers and tested these skills in the presence of my educators on the job. As a young boy, Jesus was mentored by his earthly father Joseph, and these skills equipped our Lord for service when he began his earthly ministry as a young man. This is, at its core value, what BIVO is all about. Equip-Train-Release laymen into service for God through Life on Life experience.

Community: One of the primary benefits of this type of ministry is that it involves community in a way that draws people to Christ. "I have made you a light for the Gentiles, that you may bring salvation to the ends of the earth" (Acts 13:47). And when the Gentiles heard this, they began rejoicing and glorifying the Word of the Lord, and as many as were appointed to eternal life believed. As a tradesman, I know that a good word of mouth about your skills is better than all the advertising you can invest in, because the proof is in the pudding. Your actions alone, and if necessary with words later, draws interest in your belief system. Vocational ministry meets the physical need, encounters others in a goodwill effort as a servant, and demonstrates that you care about them. Then they will listen to you.

Care for the family: Many pastors and their families learn to go without necessary everyday basics or the extras of life. While it teaches humility and promotes a penitent life, we do not need to nor are we called to be imitators of Francis of Assisi and live a life of poverty. Scripture teaches us that as our bodies are like clay pots. These pots were formed by the master potter and are for both noble and ignoble purposes. It is a noble thing to be a caretaker of property, land, and businesses or as owners and overseers like Boaz, who allowed for gleaning. Bivocational ministry profits help augment the family budget and address discretionary expenses that come up when raising a family. There will always be the unseen event that stretches a limited budget – the X Factor as I call it.

Pastors become real: We demonstrate a willingness to sweat, bleed, show emotion, and most importantly fulfil a contractual obligation with and for the client. If we do not demonstrate our giftedness in a painting or carpentry project, for instance, then

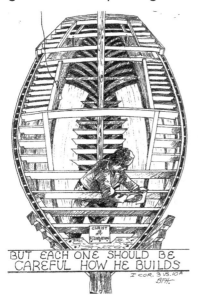

BUT EACH ONE SHOULD BE CAREFUL HOW HE BUILDS.
I COR. 3 VS. 10A
BFH.

chances are the client won't take the time to listen to our theology either. Bivocational ministry only works if we can do the work in a professional manner. This is a win if all sides are satisfied with the effort. Talk is cheap and time is short, so you will win the admiration and the ear of an unbeliever if the approach is on a level they understand. Working to reconcile the four foundational relationships with God, Self, Others, and the rest of Creation, a bivocational pastor becomes real. He can help people fulfill their callings of glorifying God by working and supporting themselves and their families with the fruit of that work.

PROCESS

Out of the box: n often-overlooked secret about trade schools or programs that teach a skill and vocation is that the student spends less and more rapidly engages his community than does a traditional college student. Whether we imitate an internship or an externship model, the classroom is in the field, in the marketplace where a skill set is needed. A student can get a financial benefit from bivocational ministry in ways that help them abstain from "school debt" which is carried for years after college. If you mix this type of training with GATEWAY (Theological Training 101) and connect the pastor in training at a district level, then it's a WIN. On its own  merit, vocational training is a timing issue, getting trained workmen to the harvest field quicker. More WINS are these facts: little or no fundraising as a traditional missionary is needed, on-the-job training as a theologian is included, as is a platform to test the skill sets are acquired and mastered.

Near Sutton, Alaska there is a training center called King Ranch.[17] They specialize in preparing a bush pilot/missionary for ministry duty. Each student learns how to fly, how to repair or even rebuild a motor, and maintain an aircraft. Most of the planes are donated, and there is a campus where students can stay while studying for exams.

The skill sets they walk out with are exactly what they need to be successful and thrive on the field. Oh, and by the way, the costs for their education are greatly reduced because of the trade school environment. This is a Christian organization offering a trade school education for men and women in Alaska, where there are more registered small aircraft than cars. Job placement is 100%, as many of the students go on the serve in aviation ministry somewhere in the world. We all remember the film *Tip of the Spear*, where the missionaries made contact by air with remote tribal people. The ability of the missionary to fly his plane in a circle, with a long lanyard and a bucket of provisions, was the first encounter with the natives. The skill sets required to perform that kind of maneuver are taught at King Ranch. On our flight over a glacier, we needed to turn back due to inclement weather, and the rain was upon us before we landed. As I was sitting in the front seat with the pilot, he touched down on a slick grassy field, and by his skill we eventually came to a stop. But don't kid yourself, the danger was real. Could we even get stopped? The young man did very well, and we were all thankful for his ability and training. Excerpts from the King Ranch website:

> Everyone working at Kingdom Air Corps is a volunteer, coming to further the vision of sharing the Gospel through the means of aviation – whether that individual is a pilot or not.

> Our volunteers do all kinds of work. They build cabins, give flight instruction, lay pipe, drive heavy equipment, clean and maintain the facility, and cook meals. This past summer, the kitchen crew prepared over 15,000 meals. Their attitude toward life is mark of obedience to the Lord, and shows a humble spirit.

> On our BCDG (Brown Church Development Group) building sites, it was expected that any

superintendent overseeing their projects would be a working super. We operated on the site with our bags on-ready to fill in wherever needed. We used the broom as well as the phone or a pen. Many hands make light work, and the goal is never personal its always corporal. Thinking of others as better than yourself, is a great team spirit attitude.

PRECIPITATE

HOW TO DO IT: "Unless the Lord builds the house, those who build it labor in vain" (Ps 127:1).

First step: Pray for the laborers of the harvest, those already in our midst in our congregations and social network who demonstrate character as persons of peace. Seek persons of influence and befriend them. This begins the **"precipitation"** process, that is-the compaction and refinement of the soil (person) we are building up. Discover whether the student has a knack or capacity at (becoming a professional "Painter, Carpenter, Cabinet maker, Flat work or Monolithic Concrete expert, Mathematical or engineering skill, Landscaping artist, Roofer, drywaller, Plumber, Electrician, Lumbermen, Tile setter, carpet layer, glass cutter, furniture builder, Artist, Mechanic for small engines or for larger advanced types. Primarily this is a "Blue Collar" skill set program that can be done as a **"self-employed"** laborer. Most pastors are considered **self-employed** in the EFCA.

The next step is for a journeyman or master tradesmen-willing to use semi or unskilled personnel on a Bid project. The client has been chosen by the teacher/trainer and the details of the finances have been established a just wage for services rendered. The project is launched, and the student is taught and tested, and proved. Assuming all is well, there is a hope of proficiency and interest, the master then advances the student to a project in which it becomes a partnership adventure. They no longer work for an hourly wage, rather they bid a project-accomplish and complete the criteria desired by the client. If all goes well- the student begins to receive deeper theological training, and if not already occurring in the process, they use their new platform to establish

71

relationships and lead a bible study group with the marketplace workers or clients they serve. Again, they must demonstrate a proficiency in the skill/trade and the ability to share the gospel in holistic ways. The latter comes at a slower pace perhaps and runs into years, but developing community and repeating this process is the goal. The Apostolic missionary /tradesman moves on and seeks another "Timothy" but stays connected as an observer to each disciple-in various ways-including prayer-co bidding a larger project, meeting in a local congregation, and sharing in fellowship.

Where to do it: Look for persons of peace in under resourced areas that exist in nearly every city in America-in places like the hood, Low rent neighborhoods, high crime areas. Be-friend them and get to know them, develop relationship and a basis of trust. The search for good material can begin in a church but Industrial plants, strip malls, city centers also can reap good people. The Bible mentions Flea markets perhaps where children run free Matthew 11:16,17. Building furniture or craft items that sell at outdoor mar-kets-you can enter this community by having a booth with sale items. Approach the children and appeal to working parents there by telling bible stories and doing art projects with children-all the while selling your hand made craft. Most markets run concurrently and are connected to a larger community of crafters-so you could travel to different communities

and stay in touch while producing product out of a garage or shop. Search listings for HOA's in your city and inquire about advertising "handy Man" services or carpentry and painting needs. Get acquainted with people of influence who direct covenant agree-ments with homeowners. Part of the role of the BIVO Pastor is to keep seeking clients who will fund this ministry, so Lumber Yards and Paint shops become a great source of connection and networking. Other market areas could include Farming communities during the harvest period, or city refuse and cleanup efforts after a weather event, such as flooding or wind damage. Insurance agencies that cover fire damaged homes-rely on contractors willing to come in and do the dirty work of clean up. But Bi-Vocational ministry within the marketplace, also requires good people skills and trained clergy/laymen and women. A marketplace solution for pastors who need to work hard at studying, should chose a support method of making items in the garage at home. One idea I plan to institute is artistic furniture such as a butcher block (Spanish styles or contemporary) for the kitchen.

I could easily develop a unique line of these tables and integrate bivo pastors into the mix-who knows they could become owners of the craft and I would simply take a small royalty.

What Is A Win?

- Short term goals realized.
- When we refine gold, and bring out a diamond in the rough.
- Lay persons step up.
- Financials improved.
- People brought to Christ.

- The church expands its territory.

- When we help facilitate a change in the cultural norm, though innovation, invention, and discovery of God's word by those who don't attend church.

Bivocational pastors demonstrate a willingness to go where God is at work. Like it says in Proverbs 12:14, "Fruit may come from his mouth, but it is the work of his hands that comes back to him." Or Proverbs 1:31, "Therefore they shall eat the fruit of their way, and have their fill of their own devices." And Proverbs 14:14, "The backslider in heart will be filled with the fruit of his ways, and a good man will be filled with the fruit of his ways." Also Job 34:11, "For according to the work of a man he will repay him, and according to his ways he will make it befall him."

The Badlands

Somewhere south of Wall, South Dakota, between Interior and Wasta, Mike Heller and I built a wilderness trail. We were assigned by Mousel Construction, an 8A contractor to develop a two-mile hiking trail into the land of badlands tundra and wildlife. Mike and I met while we both worked for the Flaig brothers company in Rapid City – he was one of my mentors and we both knew how to build staircases in all types of scenarios. I worked with Wayne, Cecil, Mike and Milton Flaig on many staircase installations. Some were quite grand in appearance (eight-foot-wide, cascading around two times before connecting to the landing above. Some were special installations, such as the refurbished staircase from a Deadwood, South Dakota casino in the 1800s, put into a custom home we built. That one Cecil and I did together, and it was magnificent, with nearly thirty steps and all those turned down spinals/balusters with a fancy top-rail. Another type I have done on a commercial site was in an enclosed elevator shaft, where your tread points were marked on a chalk line from landing to landing with seven to eight steps between each one to the fourth floor.

The wilderness project demanded creativity for nearly every step. It would have its beginning not far from the parking area on a ridge or hill that overlooked the rugged terrain below in the valley. We encountered deep ravines, arroyos, tall grass, and buffalo! It was to follow a pre-marked route and terminated in a grassy prairie setting on an octagon-shaped deck about five feet above the ground. The tourist or hiker needed a safe pathway, so asphalt gravel was used in flat areas and any steps had to be built with treated timber.

My father-in-law Milt taught me to use a piece of siding for a pattern before cutting the stringers in a zig zag shape in case I made a mistake. He also informed me how "A Good Carpenter can fix his mistakes." The crucial measurement is the height and the distance from the point of the landing down to the second point of intersection or plane. It matters if the staircase needs to terminate before nine feet or twelve feet, for instance, because that tells you what the tread width needs to be. But typically, the standard is a seven-and-a-half-inch rise (not more than that) with a nine-inch tread. I learned to mark the distance on a board, and then use my tape at seven-and-a-half inches and mark each spot

like a stitching until I got close to the objective mark (the distance). This method allows you to count the treads and number them, even though of course you could do the math, but the visual approach is important in making stairs. The remaining distance, such as three inches, can then be divided into the number of steps, such as one-eighth can now be added to each rise, giving you a seven-and-five-eighths rise. Pretty simple, right?

So, the technique is to place a tread/riser clamp for the rise at the seven-and-five-eighths mark on the tongue of the framing square, and then the other tread/riser clamp on the nine-inch mark on the body (the two-inch wide by twenty-four-inch framing square). Then you mark the triangles, each one connecting to the next until you have the correct number of treads corresponding with the height of the platform. The trick is to remember to cut one-and-a-half inches off the bottom and drop one-and-a-half inches at the top so all steps will be level and equal after you install the new tread board.

On the wilderness trail, Mike and I needed to modify the numbers to create a gentler slope in several areas, especially in bridge-style applications over a ravine. We used a dry line to mark our slope and path before installing four-by-four posted towers, some as tall as fifteen feet out of the ground. The laborers would dig the holes and fill with concrete as Mike and I proceeded though the layout work.

The tools we used are somewhat outdated by today's standards, since no such thing as a battery-operated drill had yet been introduced. We carried "brace and bit" hand drills, multiple handsaws, wood chisels, and used corded power tools with gasoline-operated generators. We used nails mostly as our fastening system, long bolts for beam and post connections, and various types of mortise and tendon or dato cuts to make our fits. I call the nailing phase of installing treads or putting beams together the "Power by Arm Strong" phase. Yes, we had good arms built up by muscle developed by pounding nails for years on end. A sixteen-penny smooth box of galvanized nails was our main stay, but we also used twenty-penny nails, and typically a sixteen-ounce or twenty-ounce hammer. Our nail bags were full and heavy, and we also carried nail pullers, chalk boxes, nail sets, utility knives, pencils, band aids, candy bars, and beef jerky in our tool pouches. And yes, the old standby Stanley thermos with a day's supply of black coffee. Mike and I also smoked Swisher sweet cigars, usually towards the day's end out in the field. I remember his ashtray was always full of the butts and used tips. Of course, neither of us would be out on the trail without a personal firearm, whether a ranch rifle or pistol, just in case. Mike carried a Colt army model .45-caliber; I carried my .41 magnum Ruger Red Hawk.

My personal skill saw, the first one I ever purchased in 1970, was an 8.5 blade size, not typical by today's standard, which is 7.5 blade size. It was a heavy worm-drive style and I used it daily for years, but now it sits on a bookshelf in my office for looks only.

The Big Horn Sheep

One morning as Mike and I pulled up to the project site, the sun was just coming up and we parked near an overlook. I said to Mike, "I think I'll stretch my legs" and walked about a hundred yards to the edge of a cliff and could see for a quarter of a mile in either direction. Below me about sixty yards away stood a big horn sheep with its head down, nearly motionless. The scene was not exactly normal –wild animals usually run from a man – but this one seemed unable to do anything but hang its head. I pondered my next move. The rock I chose was about two inches in diameter and I chose my spot, just in front of the beast, and made a good throw. As the rock landed it had the desired effect. Suddenly, the sheep backed up and then fell on its hind quarters. It was literally sitting like a dog for a few moments before tipping over like it was dizzy, and plop! It was on its side but was now awake and it began to engage its back legs, scraping itself in a round circle, unable to raise its massive horns and turn over or get up. When it stopped turning, I jogged back to Mike to inform him of the situation (but opting not to share about the stone). Mike got on the walkie talkie radio and called the Wasta Station of Engineers to report the sick and in-distress animal.

They showed up in force! You could see the line of utility vehicles coming and the dust-up they raised on the dry road coming in. Four trucks, and about a dozen men and women gathered at the edge of the cliff and we gave them our brief report. There was more radio traffic and soon there came a Huey Guard Chopper with even more operatives — special forces type guys — able to do rappelling on rocks and such. We were asked for some steel concrete stakes to secure their ropes and three men went down into the ravine. By the time they made it to the bottom, another helicopter arrived — this one was from KOTA NEWS — and they hovered about all the action, getting eye witness and first-hand video footage. It was really quiet a scene! Mike and I could hardly pay any attention to our work.

The three men were now at the downed creature, and reported back by radio that it appeared to be a rattlesnake bite on the nose, and the animal was going to be ok. They gave it a shot of medicine

and water, then stood it up on its own. As we all watched, it slowly began to walk away, to our cheers of happiness! If I remember correctly, Steve and Ralph Mousel arrived about that time to see what all was happening.

Later, when all the dust had settled, Mike and I lit up a swisher sweet cigar and poured a cup of coffee before leaving the job site for the day. Then I shared with him about the stone I threw and how it landed right in front of the creature. Mike and I figured that in retrospect, I had saved the big horn sheep's life. A weak animal in the wild won't last long with predators around. Being a carpenter always seems to bring me adventure and some sort of problem to solve. It's about learning what common sense is. They don't teach this stuff in classrooms, do they?

Glorious Grace Giftshop at Victory Bible Camp in Sutton, Alaska

Leasha and Dennis (D&L), who have a long background as church people in the EFCA, have been at this location for five years or more. They are self-supported missionaries working in a bivocational model to assist/augment the Victory Camp with its monthly budget. Glorious Grace (GG) has its own budget and the camp has its own. The camp averages 3,000 visitors each year, and Alaskan locals supply the bulk of the sale items in the gift shop. Severely handicapped children make some of the gift items as well. D&L work long hours, but a share of their time is spent each day in Christian counseling with anyone who comes with a troubled heart. The training aspect, and why this model fits a BIVO Pastor model, is that D&L teach life skills to young people. Last year 690 youth came for various conferences and worked with D&L. Job skills taught included dusting, buying products, traveling for products, cash register operation, displaying the crafts, organizing the stock room and show room, cleaning floors, accounting work, running the coffee shop, and choping firewood. Teaching these life skills is key for the youth who work there so that later, after their education in school, they can get jobs easier. Leasha works with at least three trainees (thirteen-eighteen years old) at a given time for eight weeks steady through the summer season. The efforts have greatly contributed to the success of the shop, which is known throughout the region. Both have shared God's truth, practiced Life on Life teaching, and modeled authentic community.

STORIES FROM THE FIELD

HANNANT CONSTRUCTION TRAINED YOUNG men in the art and skill of carpentry for over three decades. A pastor in the EFCA many years ago called me a tradesman in the spirit of Bezalel as described in Exodus 35:30-35. Being gifted in many types of craftsmanship and able to teach, it makes sense that bivocational ministry is something in my wheelhouse. In 2016, the goal and passion for me was to train up good-skilled and real pastors who might display the spirit of Bezalel and Caleb (Numbers 14:24). I believe in self-employment, and a pioneer spirit within the body of the church. As stated before, this type of ministry is not a replacement of the traditional church model. If anything, it assists and builds up the body of believers, equips the saints for service, and answers the call for laborers to the harvest.

So my plan was to begin seeking out clients with large enough projects to bring into play one or two BIVO prospect helpers per project. These projects have key components or principles I would teach, such as Idea, Model, Foundation, Build, Maintenance, and Bid processes mixed with theology or missional applications. The raw material and resources are already in our midst in the form of custom homes, medium-sized commercial projects and church development and remodeling projects.

Each of the key components above mentioned are topical titles that have a unique significance I'd enjoy fleshing out in greater detail than I do in this book.

Again, when proficiency has been tested and proved, a BIVO pastor moves out of the way and allows the new tradesmen to fly on his own. We become coaches who are on the sidelines and not in the game as a position player. Theological training continues, and the new student is invited into a network of pastors/tradesmen who will sharpen their skills even deeper.

By the way, in case of an environmental crisis or natural disaster, the church body who supports this type of ministry could have a ready-made crew to respond to needs. Or for future potential at the very least, the local church can display a list of skilled church people who can be a "first call" option in the community for all kinds of handyman needs. One-anothering at its best! Not second-class preachers.

It is God's prerogative to send ministers. He only can qualify men and women for and incline them to the work of the ministry. But the competency of this qualification and the sincerity of the inclination needs to be submitted to the most able judges. When the Holy Spirit is present in a multiplication movement, all the key factors (headship, one-anothering, leadership, authentic community) work to prove first-class pastors.

Was Lazarus, a poor man covered with sores, a second-class preacher? Did the rich man in this story from Jesus ask for a first-class preacher to go and tell five brothers about the gospel? Was the good Samaritan a first-class or second-class preacher when the Levite and the Pharisee ignored the man in need? Was Philip a first-class or second-class evangelist to the Ethiopian or did it matter if he was either? Did John the Baptist frequent synagogues and temples to reach the lost? No, he was called the greatest man that ever lived by the Son of God, and we all know where his mission field was. He was a man who knew Jesus well. My point is made in Romans 10:15 – "And how can anyone preach unless they are sent? As it is written: 'How beautiful are the feet of those who bring good news!'" The quote in the verse is from Isaiah 52:7.

The Soldiers at Reynosa and Saltio

The DAYA girls story earlier is as good a place as any to begin this story about two important and memorable encounters with soldiers in Mexico. Pastor Jose Nolasco and I drove from Mexico City to Reynosa for the purpose of getting eleven sewing machines sitting at the crisis response facility in Galveston, Texas. I left Jose with Pastor Benjamin in Matamoros and rented a car to drive to Galveston. My Nissan Pathfinder had federal district license plates and would have been a potential problem in the drive over to Galveston. The machines were a donation from Reach Global to the DAYA foundation, I returned to Benjamin's home with eleven of them, and met Jose for one last night of sleep before our early morning departure back to the federal district.

We left at 5AM, while it was still dark, and if all went well we would be in Mexico City by around 7PM that evening. Seventy clicks south of Reynosa, trouble was waiting for us on the highway in the dark. Suddenly, our the high beams revealed sixteen cartel soldiers dressed in camo (blue and black and gray), holding AK-47s, so we knew those were not federal agents, they were cartel thugs. Using their flashlights and waving their weapons, they brought us to a stop in the road. Jose and I spoke a few words to each other before we were commanded to exit the car: "Be calm, drink our coffee, and pray." The squad divided, one group motioned us at gunpoint to step far away from the vehicle and the rest of them ransacked our car. They took everything out and laid it on the road. When that group returned, we found ourselves surrounded in a circle with guns on us. The leader began to question "What about the eleven sewing machines?" While calmly drinking our coffee, we explained the mission to supply the girls with a training tool. We explained how we were pastors, and about our work in Mexico as Christians, the importance of teaching a skill set to the girls. They looked satisfied and walked back into the brush out of sight. We stood motionless for a minute or so, and went back to the Pathfinder to pick up the parts and pieces on the road and get ourselves out of there as fast as possible. The ordeal lasted about thirty minutes. I was not as calm as Jose, and soon at pre-dawn we took a wrong turn and found ourselves in the city of Monterrey. Looking for a route south to San Luis Potosi, we encountered a police force roadblock. There had been a hit on a nightclub that morning, a running gun battle and bombs had destroyed the club. We found ourselves experiencing a war zone because further south about an hour later we encountered 200 Federals at a local buffet where we ate breakfast. I kidded Jose, "Hey look at the bright side, you could preach here. We have a captive audience!" We were sitting at a table with armed military.

The takeaway: We accepted our fate. If God wills we should die at the hands of the armed men we encountered, then we do so testifying in the name of Jesus. It did occur to me more than once since those encounters that I might have lost my life, but God showed me His presence and protection.

Saltio

Honestly, this story is not one that I had prayed for, rather it was one I prayed against. Please Lord, don't send me to Africa – the Jonah complex, if you will – I don't want to engage anyone, just allow me to get to the US border with no incident. Literally, it was my last day in Mexico. Our little dog Bella was at my side and the Pathfinder was packed. I left at 2AM, unable to sleep through the night, wanting to get north of San Luis Potosi by lunch time. So far so good. I made a quick stop for fuel, food, and a bathroom break and continued north, thanking God for an easy trip on Route 57 North to Nuevo Laredo. Just north of Matehuala on the way to Saltio there was a military checkpoint. The cars were diverted into a coned-off pathway, and I rolled up to a squad of soldiers who took one look at me and stopped me. Instead of an easy wave and a nod, they indicated I was going to be inspected. Pull over and get out of the vehicle, they commanded. Again, as with the cartel, several soldiers held me at gunpoint and one sergeant began to ask me questions. *The first question:* Who are you and what are you doing in Mexico? Before I share my answer, allow me this brief point of interest: Don't we as believers all need to be able to answer this question? Aren't we told in scripture to be able to give a reason in season and out for the reason for our faith? It's in 2 Timothy 4:2. Therefore, even though I was not in the mood, it was a question being put to me by a man with a gun in his hand. So I answered: "I am an evangelical pastor and I work in Mexico City." He looked at me and said, "Prove it!" *Second question:* Where is your bible? Now this was classic, because my bible was stowed away in a box in the back, and I did not know which box it was in. But quickly thinking, and the words are not mine at this point because I have read where the Lord teaches us that not to worry what you are to say when put to the test for The Lord will give you the words, I answered, "My bible is in back in a box but I have my diary beside me and I can read to you something I wrote in it called the Engle Scale. The sergeant told me to continue. In Spanish, my answer looked like this: "Este escala de Engle es una medida, del conocimiento del evangelio." Translation: "This is called the Engle scale and it measures a person's knowledge of the gospel." It reads from the bottom up, ends with a person receiving the gift of salvation. For example, a negative eight on this scale indicates you have a consciousness of a supreme being but have not heard nor understand the good news. The next level, a negative seven, shows a person has been introduced to the gospel but does not receive it as a gift. As I mentioned a few more levels on the scale, standing there under guard, the other two soldiers were leaning in and listening. After reading four or five of the levels that indicate when a person is ready to receive Christ as their savior, I asked a question to the sergeant. *The third question* came from me: "Sir, where are you at on the Engle Scale? What is your response to God's word?" He looked at me, and the other two had slight smiles on their faces, and his next words were: "Okay, you can go."

A few years ago, *Christianity Today*, had an interview[18] with Dr. David Nicholas about his new book, *Whatever Happened to the Gospel?*[19] Dr. Nicholas noted how so many are defining the Gospel too narrowly, pastors tending to use their own terminology rather than scriptures, pastors preaching incomplete gospels, garbled and disjointed, pastors thinking they are preaching the bible because they encourage their people to get involved with service projects and social justice. Dr. Nichols concluded with a warning against the social gospel, moralistic teachings, and do-goodism. Perhaps these sorts of statistics have silently supported the exodus from local churches back into secular society. Still, I contend that if we go/speak/do, whether in season or out, when and where we have been called to do so, the world will slowly change one person at a time for the glory of the Lord.

An Important Historical Reference to Bivocational Ministry

In the Old testament books of Ezra and Nehemiah, three main characters (Zerubbabel, Ezra, and Nehemiah) are all leaders of the nation of Israel. These three men led groups of the remnant of Israel back into the Palestine region in the years following captivity, where the heartland of the Jews is located. Persian and Jewish history is fascinating when taken in the context of building up and developing the region. While the Persians were probably motivated by the desire to have someone else rebuild Palestine, it made sense that they used skilled craftsmen from the Jewish nation. The Persians sought to make it a source of future revenue, but the impact on the Jews was to reinvigorate their faith and stimulate them to reconstruct the temple in Jerusalem. When observed in total panorama view, does this not appear to be a bivocational model? Who can refute the building of the walls of Jerusalem with the opposition causing a worker to don a sword and a hammer? The sword for protection and the hammer for construction. Or what else can we say about Joppa, a city of commerce that became a launching place for the exponential spread of the Gospel? By the way, the work of the hands develops skill and expertise. Who wouldn't want a chair, or a table built by our lord Jesus before his ministry began? Wow! Such craftsmanship it would be!

Stanley and Livingston, the missionaries to Africa mentioned earlier, focused on specific key results areas (KRAs) to advance the gospel. Their key result areas enhanced commercial and colonial expansion by opening waterways and develop entrepreneurial enterprise. They sought the source of the Nile River but wanted to open trade routes and were anti-slavery crusaders. Their work in 1871 Africa led to the founding of several central missionary initiatives in place yet today.

Bivocational ministry is not new to the EFCA, as we can go back into its history with founding fathers and discover how tradesmen pastors were the norm. In 2003-2004 at the EFCA home office, Karla and I were candidates for missionary status along with Bill Ahern and his family from North Dakota. The EFCA sent Bill into China (a closed-access country) as a "weed scientist" with KRAs that intermingled with financial profit for both he and the Chinese. This approach to reach the lost is not an unknown strategy for building the Kingdom of God.

While I was in Mexico City, I helped initiate two water purification plants for the two churches we started. There was an immediate holistic gospel impact in an underdeveloped neighborhood near a major metro station. Like some cities in the world, streets and byways can be in hilly areas, not flat or level. Literally, a colonia (neighborhood) could be a five-to-ten-block area and able to keep to itself with an OXXO (a brand of convenience store) or a mini market or a tianguis (farmer's market or flea market) in the street. People had limited finances to get water into their homes, so a local water plant within walking distance was a godsend. The first church invested in a tri-bike with a large basket to carry the water jugs and deliver to various homes. Oh yes, and passing out a "chic" or tract "AGUA REY" with a bible verse made an impact. It built relationships and met a physical need. The second plant was eventually sold to a third church group that has been thriving with this water works in a very poor area in southern Mexico City.

Here is the "genesis" of the water purification plants for the tiny churches: They were a success at different levels of measurement according to their cultural context. Like any business model, time and patience is needed in seeing a mature development of the business. If we apply typical BIVO principles, we know they don't get a pass at each juncture of the business or the training. Instead, they had to work through the kinks and issues that presented themselves and solve them. They discovered their weaknesses and their strengths and were given flexible time constraints. My expectations were of approximately three years to be at full production mode based on equipment potential and ownership in the project.

Water Mission[20] in Charleston, South Carolina in the year 2010 provided initial data I needed for basic plants. I read about emergency solutions for water purification in Honduras in 2001, which led to entrepreneurship, and even delved into the use of solar power to handle the pumps needed. In Charleston, Water Mission shipped 120 units of the smaller cage variety plants to Haiti, at about $900 each. But the idea for a sustained and larger tank supply would require a more sophisticated system. In Mexico City, I found a company that produces plants capable of making 500 "garaphons" (about a four-gallon bottle) per day. Inmaculada in the south of the city not only had the gear and equipment, but they also trained people in its use, and certified plant managers. Of course, I introduced each church and staff to the company and sat in on several trainings with them. We had the resources at our fingertips, all we needed was funding. Dan Jenkins, a missionary in Costa Rica, assisted with a financial and funding plan. A trip to Kansas with supporters yielded a great contact for me: An Economics Professor at Notre Dame who happened to be a grandson of one our individual supporters, and he worked out a tax strategy and market analysis for the idea. Representatives of the two churches signed a contract that stated, in part: $6200 USD would be raised for each plant, and the money did not have to be returned because it was a seed gift.

I worked out a plan to house the equipment based on each Church's context. In the Case of REY Church, they needed to remodel an existing room with access to the street. We talked about transportation of the finished product, sales, paychecks for the workers, and who was going to take "ownership" in the church body.

There was a different model for the plant in the south. In the case of Vida Abundante, it was to be located in an unchurched, unreached people group, and two couples from the church were going to relocate and live there. But eventually it was sold to the working couple who then joined another church forming in the area. Today, that little plant is thriving, but again changed hands to another local believer. For me, the life lesson learned for this daring strategy to grow the church body was "who will take ownership?" It was frustrating in the beginning, trying to open their eyes to the possibilities, which took time, but the effort was rewarded. For both churches, the answer to their dilemma was to recruit individuals from the outside who had a desire and giftedness for entrepreneurial spirit. This step in the development of a BIVO person is the part where the trade is passed on to another capable set of hands.

The old saying "You can lead a horse to water but you can't make him drink" is true with people and horses and a "novice" you are attempting to form into a rock-solid believer in Jesus who will be well rounded and grounded in maturity.

A bivocational pastor must be a businessman of sorts, and he must wear several hats. It is not for the faint of heart. But past saints and a lot of empirical evidence demonstrate there can be long-term positive effects on community and Church from this type of pioneer work. I am reminded of the missionary John Williams, who was called the Messenger of Peace. Before he began his missionary journey, John built his own ship. He sailed from Raiatea in 1830 in a vessel of between sixty and seventy feet that he had built with his own hands without skilled assistance, without any training in shipbuilding, and with only a few simple tools at his disposal. If God could do that for him, then God will provide the tools and resources for entrepreneurial church planters and Kingdom-growing servants.

February 2010 New Orleans Crisis Response

Long after the water had receded in the city of New Orleans, there was an ongoing discovery process to meet potential clients and understand their needs. Thelma was a name on a list for me as I sat in the office of Crisis Response going over projects. Karla and I literally had dropped our home assignment efforts to raise support for a Mexico ministry and joined the front lines of the ongoing Katrina relief work. On this particular day (helping out Mark Lewis, who was in Haiti), I was in a planning mode before outside teams arrived, and the task at hand was a detailed drawing of an exterior staircase on a two-story building. Thelma's project required a permit from the City Desk, so after preparing a fax I called the city building inspector's office. Soon I was speaking with a gentleman named Gary (not his real name) and introduced

APOSTLES TEACHING BREAKING BREAD PRAYER

myself as an EFCA missionary with Crisis Response. It was his job to approve these drawings I had made of the two-story staircase and fire escape project. I asked a simple question during a pause in our conversation: Do you own a property in the city and how badly was it damaged? He said, "As a matter of fact I do, and have a long way to go on it. The work has been tiring and has taken me almost a year now, but I have no one to help me." I said, "Gary, do you realize this is what we do here at the EFCA? Our base is in Covington, but we work all over the city doing humanitarian aid projects. Can we help you?" It quickly got really quiet, and then he answered, "Are you serious"? I said, "Give us an address and a time to meet with you and we will come to you." Again, this was one of the city managers who was so busy coordinating recovery efforts for others he had little time or labor resources for his own home. He and I had discussed the fact that there were many shady, fly-by-night contractors who were abusing the poor folks in the flood-ravaged areas of New Orleans. Who can you trust to do the work, when evidence of fraudulent contractors could be found in every quadrant of the city? This opens the door for ethical, honest tradesmen/bivocational men and women to shine in a new light, building trust and performing in creative ways.

We did meet with Gary, and we began a fruitful relationship over the next year. He discovered that the hands and feet of Jesus exist, and God cares about him and loves him. Networking is an amazing tool, and we discover that when we show an interest in another human being, they then will show an interest in what we as believers care about. Ministry in the everyday marketplace looks like this. It places us away from the pulpit and in the center of God's will on the field of battle. And we know that Jesus is always entering, always moving toward occupied territory, always engaging the stranger, and always demonstrating a will to recapture stolen ground.

We were not second-class workers in New Orleans, as Ms. Pat found out, as well as Gary. Because of the amount of debris inside a home, teams of volunteer workers became experts in "de-breeding." My wife Karla led a women's volleyball team from John Brown University into Ms. Pat's home, and those women worked passionately to "gut" the bad stuff. Ms. Pat had been called into action as an army sergeant to keep order at the Dome for almost a year, neglecting her own home. Karla and I listened to her story and connected her to the Crisis Response team, and the ladies from John Brown were amazing when they sprang into action! It was a win-win!

The Walls in Matamoros

The year was 2001, and the location was one of if not the poorest areas along the border of Mexico. Juan Roque (Pastor of the Las Palmas Church) challenged our vision team (five midwest churches, McCook, Alliance and Sidney EFC) to do a humanitarian work between Matamoros and Reynosa, Mexico. The Torchbearers International and RIO Grande Bible College would become players in a project to build a twenty-by-forty two-story church building. Eric and June Petersen coordinated the plans as RG missionaries on the Mexico side, and I directed our Sidney EFC team, beginning with meetings on strategy and skill sets with the six chosen men. During the eight weeks prior to our arrival, Eric and June coordinated the Torchbearers in laying the concrete slab. I met with our chosen men and poured into them the strategy and process of how to get this building raised. Each man knew his role on the team, and we all knew each other's designated tasks as well, in case we lost a man for whatever reason. This building pad was only fifty feet from the Union Pacific Railroad track and behind the Purina Dog Chow factory, and it was badly out-of-square.

By the way, just as an aside, the training students get when they enroll in the Torchbearers International College is a blend of hands-on and classroom teaching. Whether or not the students perfect the skills it takes to pour a concrete slab is not exactly the goal. The goal is to be the hands and feet of Jesus and go. Matthew 9:13 – "Go and learn what this means: 'I desire mercy, not sacrifice.' For I have not come to call the righteous, but sinners."

The first miracle: On the Sunday evening before a Monday start for the construction, a prayer request came up before the team and congregation at Las Palmas Church. A man needed type B-positive blood for a surgery he had been waiting to have. A man on our team had the B-positive blood type, so he elected to go to the hospital for three days to donate his blood during the surgery. *The second miracle*: Down one man already, two of our teammates took ill from food poisoning and we found ourselves with only three men from our team to start the project. However, God provided about fifteen Mexican men during the first day of work. These men wanted to learn how to work with wood and build a structure with something other than a cement block. Perhaps they desired to learn as much as they could so as to put the new skills to use earning a living. *The third miracle:* The two walls we had built were also sheathed not only with oriental strand board (OSB) but also stone siding panels, which made them about a thousand pounds each. To raise them we needed a lot of muscle power, and God provided! enter RIO GRANDE Bible students who happened to be in the area. The extra manpower did the trick and we raised the walls with ease. *The fourth miracle:* When the old shack was torn down (formerly a place for drug users and prostitutes to get help for addictions), the local witch rejoiced in the street a block away around a fire she had built. But she soon was quieted when the building was raised five days later. *The fifth miracle:* Our total construction costs came in at less than half what we had planned for. *The sixth miracle:* The women did their part as the larger work force needed food and clean clothes, so they cooked for our men each day and even washed our dirty clothes for a price. *The seventh miracle:* I thank God for the ability to visualize and foresee how things come together. For eight weeks I taught my team how to build a house, step by step, and each man knew the other's role. By the way, an important feature to bivocational ministry is that the novice learns something they can take to the next step on their own. One of the men became a contractor and developer, and flipping homes became his way of life. He was an accountant before the short-term trip to Mexico.

The eighth miracle: The rain came. When Elijah was finished at Mt. Carmel with the prophets of Baal, he girded up and ran ahead of Ahab's chariot all they back to the city. Then the rain came in torrents, and it did the same for us in Matamoros. The flooding began only hours after the last shingle was laid, and we had said our good-byes. In fact, during the flooding after our team was safely back in

Harlingen, Texas, the church we had just built became a refuge for the poor people who fled to it to avoid being swept away!

I remember making friends each day and demonstrating how to measure, hammer, make a cut, or build a section of wall, or form stairs, or build a header or the trusses we needed to make on-site. I poured myself into the men and they learned, and they did, and we accomplished the job in only four-and-a-half days. A forty-by-twenty two-story building with windows and doors and a steeple on the roof! By the way, the son of the witch who celebrated when the old shack was torn down two years earlier, unlocked the door for me when I returned to check in on ministers there. One footnote about our team: Don Tincher, a Lineman for the County of Cheyenne in Nebraska, died six months later. He never fully recovered from his sickness when we arrived in Reynosa. Our Church elders laid hands on him and prayed, then we all discovered he had cancer. But he did think the evil of the area may have had something to do with exacerbating his cancer. His wife Marion told us he died doing the very thing he felt God had called him to do: being a short-term missionary in a foreign country. It is ironic and fitting that it was his idea to build the steeple with the cross, and the Mexicans somehow got that thing up on the roof by themselves as we gringos stood by and watched.

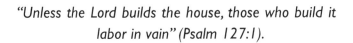

HOUSE DISCIPLESHIP

"Unless the Lord builds the house, those who build it labor in vain" (Psalm 127:1).

TWO SIMILAR CONCEPTS OF creative training build up and edify the novice in each phase of the project, which can have specific measurable impacts and results on an individual novice trying to become the master. Where does a novice today learn the value of good work?

Master Carpenter Training and Home Construction

Construction of a Custom Home

1. Idea and Plan (including budget)

While I listen to their dream, that is, "the big idea on the client's heart," it comes into focus with a sketch as we talk and present broad-stroke ideas. Okay, assuming we can approach a banquet table or, for practical purposes, a wonderful buffet of Mongolian food, cowboy BBQ, sushi, Italian, Mexican, or whatever your taste is. For a new home construction client this may translate to an HGTV dream image of a new open living space concept, with no limit on costs, with all the bells and whistles. Meanwhile, for a prospective novice desiring to learn a trade which they can launch into full time self-employment, it all depends on desire, skills/ability, opportunity, and exposure to industry standards.

What are the needs in terms of space and design for the best fit, ergonomically and budget-wise? What type of building will it be? A two-story colonial? A simple ranch style? A multilevel structure to fit the context of a sloped ground? Or perhaps a remodel of a 100-year-old house? The idea comes to life as the rough draft or profile takes shape. The "Big Idea" is tempered with stewardship, location, time, and weather. We can sketch the dream, but to transform it from paper, well that is what this book is all about.

In terms of missional objective, no contact with clients translates to Loss of Influence. The Church is to be missional, the salt and light, taking the gospel witness into the community of need. For the novice (disciple subject), do I have enough work available for deeper learning, or do I have a two-week project where we work fast, get in, get out, and make a profit? Some call it "Blow and Go" construction. Every project in a bivocational pastor's sphere of influence has four objectives: The shepherd earns a wage, the novice learns a trade, the client gains an improved living situation, and the Lord is glorified through the efforts.

Note of interest: I'm never without a sketch pad, and pen or pencil. You never know when you will need to communicate with someone using a visual aid. Likewise, for the novice we begin a series of testing and on-the-job training to determine skill, aptitude, and desire to validate a starting wage. Very key for a bivocational learner/servant/worker is their personal calling and dream. Where do they see themselves in two-to-five years? In this opening scenario, both the client and the novice get to voice their needs and I realize how I can be of service through thefour objectives. The context of a project is always different, but my core principles remain steady while methods and material change. Jesus said, "follow me and I will make you fishers of men" (Mt 4:19), and oh how different in character those twelve men were from each other! Simon, Peter, James, and John were fishermen (Lk 5:9,10), and Levi was a tax collector (Lk 5:27). Bartholomew or Nathanael, son of Talmai, lived in Cana of Galilee. He had ties with nobility or of noble birth. Tolmai or Talmai (2 Sam 3:3) was King of Geshur whose daughter Maacah was the wife of David, mother of Absolom. The fact that these different men chosen by Jesus to be his disciples already existed should be of encouragement to a BIVO pastor because our novices and clients already exist, they just need to be discovered. Therefore, a simple cursory examination of the twelve men Jesus chose teaches us to understand "unity in the midst of diversity." Bivocational ministry cuts across many lines, and there is no cookie cutter mold.

Not to belabor this point, but while I was in the field in Mexico, we identified our contacts as "Network Partners." They became a multitude of eager participants to us, including the following, though you won't recognize all of these as I'm using common names, acronyms, and abbreviations: DAYA, CCBC, YWAM, Gideons, M. Cadena, W. Testa, ASLAM, CAM, UNAM, Felipe M., PARTNERS, DNA, FIEL, ADIEL, Church Plants, TG, RG, Water Mission, Santander, Nissan, Toyota, Pentecostal Church, Betel, Free Church, ATT, Private Schools, DIF, JMM, and NGO. I also contacted the Alvaro Obregon Delegation Council, the US Embassy, and a man who became a good friend, Jose Mondragon, a water scientist who sailed with National Geographic for the government of Mexico on various expeditions.

The second meeting generally occurs many days later, after the research of pricing and square footage costs are somewhat known. The floor plan is a major focus, which aligns with the third step of context of the ground, do we have a level area to build on or is it rocky and or sloping? By this time, I have drawn more detailed lines and included measurements to prove costs, but loosely determined to see how a budget looks for the client. Typically, there is a debate of sorts and back and forth we go to determine if they have stewardship ability to bear the cost of time and expenses. If we can determine a budget with moderate changes, then the plan will be "inked" or "blued" to submit to other subcontractors. I extend the job opportunity to HVAC, electric, concrete, and lumber companies to win the bid for their respective roles. A date is set to reconvene after bids are in, and a basic plan and budget is ready for a banker. My helper and "BIVO candidate" also dialogues with respect to his commitment of time and willingness to learn. Expectations met or unmet will be an issue throughout this endeavor. In the 1970s, Flaig Construction hired Vo-Tec or trade school students for summer work. They also hired teachers who were on break from classes, and who proved to be adept in carpentry. Most of the novices or "rookies" as we used to call them, were on a different career path into related industries surrounding home construction. So, I am sensitive to the specific skill sets encountered with young individuals who in the future will excel in sales or accounting or perhaps in design fields. Luke 14:28 – "For which of you desiring to build a tower, does not first sit down and count the cost, whether he has enough to complete it?"

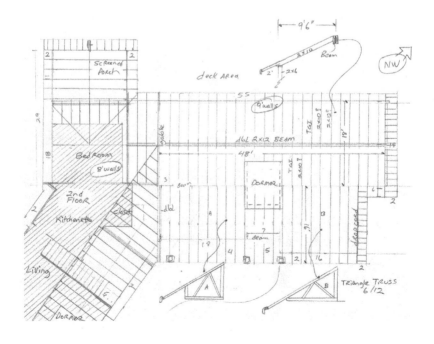

2. Ground and Foundation (the precipitate process)

In the opening scene of the epic movie *Gettysburg*, the first commanders on the field spoke about "good ground." Of course, the context was "is this a good place for a fight we can win?" On the contrary, in another scene in the same film, Robert E. Lee is quoted as saying, "It does not matter whether our opponent chooses the ground or not, we will meet him on the field of battle and take him on." As we all know, the outcome favored the generals who took heart in choosing the correct ground before beginning the campaign. Likewise, if the potter does not precipitate the clay before placing it on the wheel, he will lose the battle when the item comes under intense fire. In construction, the ground must be able to bear the weight of the building. Observe the leaning tower of Pisa, for example, or visit the Zocalo in Mexico City and experience the settling and sinking of not only the church but government offices as well. In the center inside the Cathedral in Mexico City, a giant plumb bob hangs over a center mark on the floor. The "bob" is a full meter off -center, indicating the building has settled due to weak soil composition. Matthew 7:26,27 – "And everyone who hears these words of mine and does not do them will be like a foolish man who built his house on the sand. And the rain fell, and the floods came, and the winds blew and beat against that house, and it fell, and great was the fall of it." After scouting and inspecting the building site, noting slopes and drainage, rocky or clay soil, subterranean fill (gravel type) will most likely be needed. As this sub-fill is placed it must be done so in layered, compacted levels. The goal is to achieve a ninety percent or better density rating on compaction. Certain areas in the world require frost footings at six feet deep, other areas three feet deep or less. Other areas in zone two earthquake locations, footings need to change shape (instead of rectangular, two even-sized triangles are placed side by side. This allows the ground to push between them and act as a buffer in quake events. The Alaskan pipeline footings move all the time, so a special design above ground is used, and constant inspection is required. The point is: compaction of the ground is necessary to ensure the building process will be preserved long after the project is finished. The same is true for the bivo candidate or novice, who must be vetted prior to investing a lot of time in them. Are they interested in kingdom building, are they called to it by God, and are they gifted to either learn how to or to be trained to a specific skill set?

As churches and secular institutions go, we make our belief and creed statements a concrete absolute, formed and shaped to be a fundamental rock we base our work and ministry or work ethic on. Once the ground has been "precipitated or compacted" it is this next step that can become a mistake or a blessing to the rest of the project, or (por lo menos, at the very least) not turn out as we planned.

Forming a basement, a slab or a retaining wall requires different techniques and years of skill and training to master. One of my first concrete projects where I trained with masters of the trade was a swimming pool for the Best Western Hotel in Hill City, South Dakota. Chicken wire, five-inch slump concrete (slump refers to the amount of settling of a shovel of fresh cement. If it is very wet it will slump down to one or two inches; if it is much dryer it will stay near five inches tall without receding), and a Darby wood float were used. The Mexican crew worked fast to lay the wire and form the kidney-shaped pool, seemingly from scratch. Another forming project I trained on was a 50,000-gallon water tank at Chapel Hills in Rapid City. This process required a massive footing, ten-foot-tall plywood forms and screw jacks for a "slab on deck" top cap or lid after the walls were formed and poured. Another style of forms is called "monolithic" because they change shape and are sometimes attached to another structure. One of my largest form projects was done on the Nevada Test Range where we used Simon Pans (steel frame with plywood inserts). It was a round structure about thirty feet tall and sixty feet wide with a wall opening (thickness) at twenty-four inches on all sides. These types of forms require a snap tie and cone process (wall spreaders) with strong back and whalers to keep the forms from moving. The Simon pans come in different interchangeable sizes and parts. A steel tie (different lengths depending on the width of the wall) protrudes thru the form and out the side. Two-by-four lumber is placed against the pan and a triangle shape or wedge clip slides down next to the lumber to secure the wall from exploding due to the pressure of wet concrete. We say, "It's never a mistake until it's poured." Occasionally a clip or tie will fail to hold, and you can have a zipper effect, with others failing due to the stress and pressure.

The more I considered this important step, my eyes were opened. I realized that formation of our spiritual journey can also be instrumental in the way we process information. Three different perspectives (P1, P2, and P3) can be described as follows:

P1=One-dimensional: In the visual arts field we can see images on a flat background with no shadow or depth. People can be like this; some hear and don't understand and remain one-dimensional. One-dimensional perspective is like an oxymoron in writing, because while the written word is flat, the words we use are describing something through imagination and experience. Examples of the one-dimensional are "stop signs," a target, directional arrows, labels on doors or commercial products, or the "fine print" in a contract.

P2=Two-dimensional: Art images such as photography, painting, and drawings which reveal shadows and depth are two-dimensional. For centuries artists have wowed us with their brilliance in mastering light on a canvas. When I design/build for a client, some of my first sketches will have perspective and shadowing, illustrating dimension and depth. A simple example would be to draw a square or even better a rectangle and then draw two lines intersecting the four corners, like an X, then draw a third line through the center of the X from left to right or horizontally and you have a foreground, a middle ground, and a background. Suddenly there is perspective, even without shadowing or even placing an image on the page. These types of sketches give the client a view of what is possible before even putting a shovel in the ground. Today of course there is program called 3D imaging-and beyond to Auto-Cad systems. But sticking with P2 for a moment, oh how the masters have given us perspective using color and shading such as Rembrandts portraits and Monet's landscapes. Regarding people and their spiritual formation on this level, they may achieve deeper understanding of theology but don't ever make it real in their life, remaining two-dimensional.

P3=Three-dimensional: But alas, to achieve a three-dimensional art form, we must do what God has done in the book of Genesis and create a sculpture in the round. It could be formed by a mold, or by a potter's hand on the wheel, or by removing substance that does not belong to the completed image (stone carvers), or perhaps building a home. The finished product if we are working on the development of an individual will be a person who grasps the truth of the Gospel and becomes a living testimony to the glory of God. This three-dimensional person is well rounded, able to be seen in God's image, with refined character, moral value, spiritual awakening and physically fit. Or they could be an image of a golden calf, made by disgruntled chosen people of God.

In the movie *The Patriot*, don't you feel sorry for the man in the wood shop who fails over and again to make a perfect rocking chair, able to hold his weight? He angrily throws the reject into a pile of other rejects, and I asked myself: Where is his master? Where was his training? The moral of the story is that this man was not destined for this moment in time to be a carpenter. Instead, he was needed to be a leader and fighter for freedom and independence. The lesson is this: We must be watchful for desire and skill sets in training a novice, notice what questions they ask, and notice what they get joy from doing or at times what they don't do very well.

2 Timothy 4:14,15 "Alexander the coppersmith did me great harm; the Lord will repay him according to his deeds. Beware of him yourself, for he strongly opposed our message." Matthew 21:28-31a – "What do you think? A man had two sons. And he went to the first and said, 'Son, go and work in the vineyard today.' And he answered, 'I will not,' but afterward he changed his mind and went. And he went to the other son and said the same. And he answered, 'I will go, sir,' but did not go. Which of the two did the will of his father?"

The master builder, the potter, or the portrait artist strive to create a perfect, beautiful form, but Christ's example of humility was that of a servant.

Philippians 2: 5-8 – "Have this mind among yourselves, which is yours in Christ Jesus, who, though he was in the form of God, did not count equality with God a thing to be grasped, but emptied himself, by taking the form of a servant, being born in the likeness of men. And being found in human form, he humbled himself by becoming obedient to the point of death, even on a cross."

3. The Pre-Build and Delegate

This next step in transforming a novice into a master tradesman is by changing the medium. The foundation work has been completed, set in proper perspective to east, west, north south exposure to the sun, forms are off and the foundation is backfilled. To change medium from concrete to wood or steel, a master carpenter is needed to square the mudsill to the concrete by measuring and adjusting.

What is the mudsill? It is a building platform, typically done with two new mediums (wood and fiberglass/or a perma-foam to stop gap weather and outside elements). It is firm enough to build on and attach other material to, but coupled with fiberglass it provides a sealant between concrete and the rest of the building. It must be true, level, and square. It is as important as a set of rubber tires are to a car. The skill sets are teachable and memorable – once you learn them, you will always have them in your mind. There are some skills you get so rusty at you may not ever regain the ability, specifically in the area of dexterity and physical strength. However, to use a little lingo you might hear on a construction site: "I ain't as good as I once was, but I'm as good once as I ever was." Most carpenters are humble, penitent men, doing an honorable job.

Besides the basic skills of measuring, cutting, and fitting, we now focus on the Pythagorean Theorem: The Euclidean Theorem and the Cross Check. Building the headers, cutting the cripples and short studs, culling the studs that will go into the wall, laying out the wall plates, setting the mud seal and building the beam for the main floor over the basement, all of which are learnable skills that remain with you as a master carpenter. But to square a foundation you need to understand that THE BUCK stops with you! Whatever surface, out of whack, straight, not straight, bumpy, smooth or incongruency you discover, YOU are the one that fixes it right here, right now! As Milton Flaig, my father-in-law always said, "A good carpenter will be able to fix or repair his mistakes." A good follow-up to this is what Paul Larson said in 1976 at the Robinsdale Housing project in Rapid City, South Dakota: "And a good painter will make a carpenter look great."

But I digress. The point is, you are now in control of the way this house will be crafted, crooked or not, but we prefer level and straight lines. After all, your name is going to be associated with this project! Isaiah 26: 7 – "The path of the righteous is level; you make level the way of the righteous." Proverbs 22:1 – "A good name is to be chosen rather than great riches, and favor is better than silver or gold."

With the mudsill (typically wooden or steal base) bolted to the cement foundation, your project will be "true and ready" for a precise structure. To begin: Using a 100-foot tape or longer, you measure the cement outside corners and perform a Cross Check. Measuring two diagonal distances on the square or rectangle, the correct formula for square is an equal distance in both measurements. The process gets tricky if the concrete is off by an inch or more or "out of square" as we say. This happens during the pour. Forms get bumped or a wall may be "out of level." So, the first measurement on a foundation is a half-inch in from the outside all the way around or at least on all four corners. Measure the distance and "cross check" with the Euclidean Theorem, and if is not the same measurement, adjust one corner by a half-inch and recheck until the cross check is perfect. At this point you snap a chalk line (typically blue or red) on the concrete on all four sides and use this line to verify square. This is where the Pythagorean theorem can be used to perform a smaller cross check by measuring up the line. 3A and 4B feet. The true square will be 5 feet (C), exactly on the cross check or third leg of the triangle. So again, the formula is 3/4/5 or the distance for square is between 3 & 4 and will/be 5. The variants on these numbers are (X2-times two) example; 6-8-10; 12-16-20; 24-32-40 and so on for bigger squares or rectangles to square up. But it would be enough to only need the Cross check.

Next, the mudsill is installed by measuring bolt hole placements (typically every six feet and typically a half-inch or a five-eigths diameter bolt) and drilling a three-quarter-inch diameter hole so it can be bolted to the cement. By following your square chalk line as a guide, you will be nearly done except for one more check with the tape before tightening all the bolts.

Once this is done, another level line or "dry line" (as a brick layer would use) is placed horizontally to determine a smooth level elevation around the perimeter. Using wooden shims, you tighten or loosen the nut on each bolt making slight adjustments up or down. By the way, the insulation is used like an Oreo cookie sandwich between the wood and the cement. This insures cold and hot elements will not pass through (or bugs, spiders, dirt, and so on).

At this point the next phase is ready, which is to build the glue/lam beam or set a steel I-Beam or use a T-Lam beam. The beam pockets on two sides receive the fourteen-inch tall beam down into the pocket, and are then shimmed and leveled to match the exact height of the mud sill.

The beam is set into the pockets, but an adjustable FHA jack post or screw-type post is set at ten-foot increments (sometimes two posts, sometimes three) across the length of the beam, underneath to support the beam and subfloor. Using a "dry line" pulled taught across the beam and a little above, it can be leveled by measuring the same distance at any interval. Typically, we make a beam three-eighths of an inch higher in the center to allow for settling with future weight bearing.

The Box. Another term for the "box" is a "sub band" that is nailed to the Mudsill, and it is of the same material as the joists that carry the floor. The box is fastened all the way around, and the joists are all set at sixteen inches on center and over lapping one or two feet across the center beam. All crowns are up and ready for "squaring of the box." Note: A basic skill in working with any dimensional lumber is to be able to determine its usefulness by observing if it is a straight board (culling the lumber is a common term used). Even with a slight bow, a joist can be used with its "crown" in an upward posture, allowing weight and time to settle the lumber into a level position.

With the center beam secured by diagonal bracing so it won't move, the joists now are used to hold the exterior box to "square and true" as they are fastened to the beam using two men, one on the outside measuring the dryline and the other nailing across the beam length on each joist. Ezekiel 40:3 – "When he brought me there, behold, there was a man whose appearance was like bronze, with a linen cord and a measuring reed in his hand."

As I have learned in my career, scripture is applicable to job site construction tactics, usable terminology when turning a novice into a master carpenter. The book of James chapter 1 speaks to "hearing and doing the word." "Be doers of the word, and not hearers only, deceiving yourselves" (Jam 1:22). Verse 25 –"But the one who looks into the perfect law, the law of liberty and perseveres, being no hearer who forgets but a doer who acts, he will be blessed in doing."

The pre-build & delegate phase is critical in terms of releasing a man to practice this step in becoming a master. Bivocational ministers have learned the importance of specialized skill sets.

I am reminded of a New Tribes missionary who served in Papa New Guinea years ago, Norm Frye. Norm made early contact with native tribes by helping to bring them food. His methods included riding on a motorcycle with a shot gun, chasing down wild pigs. He grew up in Nebraska, learning these useful abilities and they are absolutely skills sets that help make ministers relatable and real, outside the doors of a church building.

4. Layout and Material

Continuing with headers, short studs and culling lumber, the training and education begins to perfect and refine. The header is specifically designed to support weight across an opening, entry way, or windows. It must be built square and true, and doing so is a good task for the novice under supervision. Typically, the process begins with "culling" or the selection of non-warped, less knots, not-so-sappy and heavier timber for use in window and door headers.

Framing the structure and developing a profile, outline, and shape by enclosing, sealing up, and preparing for other building substrates that have to do with trims and finishes can all happen by providing a base to adhere to.

5. Dry-In and Infrastructure

The dry-in process is the part of the project where two-dimensional drawings become three-dimensional structures. It's the "wow" factor in the building timeline. Finally, we all get to see what all the dust-up and hub-bub is about and answer the question "What is it going to look like? Now is the time for revealing the image and craftsmanship designed for a specific client.

Imagine with me the same question about heaven, our eternal dwelling place. Jesus our Lord is busy preparing a place for us so we can be with him. Titus 2:13,14 – "waiting for our blessed hope, the appearance of the glory of our great God and Savior Jesus Christ, who gave himself for us to redeem us from all lawlessness and to purify for himself a people for his own possession who are zealous for good works." Titus 3:14 – "And let our people learn to devote themselves to good works, so as to help cases of urgent need, and not be unfruitful." Our zealous works, at this stage are paying off, and the fruit of our labor takes shape.

This is a fast-moving phase and is the part of the project that always seems to be the most vulnerable to weather. Ezekiel 19:12 – "But it was uprooted in fury and thrown to the ground. The east wind made it shrivel, it was stripped of its fruit; its strong branches withered, and fire consumed them." The walls go up (balloon frame method or "stick-built"), and in many areas of the country it is done by "piece workers." But for BIVO applications I prefer "peace workers" because it takes a stud to build a house. And the roof lines are created by "stacking the trusses," which are typically pre-builds from a plant or factory off-site. This is part of the reason I mentioned the weather, the wind always seems to blow when raising a wall, a truss, or putting on sheathing.

6. Exteriors (and Landscapes)

Coverings and substrates are the underlayments for the final clothing of the home. Typically, plywood or OSB (oriental strand board) is used, with a waterproof or wind-proof fabric. If there are valleys on a roof, metal flashing and felt (tar paper) are used prior to putting on shingles, shakes, or even a metal covering. The exterior walls will get a Tyvek wind wrap or a thermal board installed prior to siding and/or brick/stone applications. Windows and doors are installed during this phase to complete the "dry-in." The idea is to prepare for the interior work by preserving and protecting the frame and interior for the finishing products. Isaiah 61:10 – "I delight greatly in the Lord; my soul rejoices in my God. For he has clothed me with garments of salvation and arrayed me in a robe of his righteousness, as a bridegroom adorns his head like a priest, and as a bride adorns herself with jewels." Ephesians 6 speaks about putting on the armor of God, and for a home we put on the armor for the elements it will need to withstand. The client also begins to realize that a new name will appear on their address form: Perhaps the home gets a new name such as the "River House," or the "Elm Street Place," or the "Chateau on the Hill." Similarly, we look forward to a new name given to us in heaven (Revelation 3:12).

In the world of art, during the sketch and after the basic profile, the shading begins that reveals and refines the definition of the shape. It adds perspective and demonstrates where the light source is coming from. Shading brings out the splendor in the same way the dry-in phase brings out the beauty of the framed structure.

In terms of skill sets, this phase is a proving/testing for the novice, to determine if he can put his training to use at this next or higher level of craftsmanship. He is becoming a tradesman and is now capable of performing multiple tasks in carpentry.

We also will begin to understand what specific area for which the novice is well-suited, what skill has he performed well enough to venture out on his own and make a living doing? The master of marble and paint Michelangelo trained in wax formation, bronze castings, reliefs, tool making, fresco, and sketching with charcoal. The day finally came for him when he demonstrated his giftedness with the human form and his use of detail such as his PIETA carving in Rome. He was a commissioned artist for many projects because of his talent and training.

Because I performed well with siding and soffits on the exterior of the homes, Flaig brothers felt I was ready for trims and finishes such as cabinets and doors on the interior.

7. Finishes and Turnkey

By the time the inside of a custom home is ready for finishes, it has been inspected for all utilities, (electrical, plumbing, heat and air, and insulation) and has been sheet-rocked/taped, textured, and painted. I just mentioned at least eight different trades that today have become specialty contracting areas of expertise. Again, this is opportunity for the novice carpenter to see the various elements in action, maybe they appreciate one or more of them and have a leaning or tendency to learn a second trade. It happens all the time, and in retrospect I took advantage of learning from masters of tape, texture, painting and more because of *feast or famine*. Yes, tradesmen go through hard and lean times, but so do many characters in the bible. In some cases, there is a Divine Distance (think Daniel or Joseph or Esther) that brings distance between God and his subjects who are far away from their own land. In other times, God is front and center, side by side (think Noah or Bezalel). A key phrase in Exodus 35: 34 besides the fact that several skill sets are given to Bezalel, "And He (The Lord) has inspired him to teach, both him and Oholiab the son of Ahisamach of the tribe of Dan."

I have often considered this word "teach" in context of scriptural or theological instruction, but clearly it applies to many trades and skill sets as well. Have we just read a precursor or early example of bivocational ministry? I think so!

The term "finishes" is very extensive and significant of various levels of carpentry, trims, doors, cabinets, shelves, hardware, and so on. At this level, in order to be able to perform these skill sets we are using a skilled mechanic now. We are talking about a person who has proven they can handle (measure-cut-fit into place) so well they are considered experts. The dressings at this point become like a "signature" or trademark and have considerable impact on the next phase of the project (maintenance and warranty).

One short story about my transition to becoming a finish carpenter: A Rockwell or Porter-Cable door jig (which today is hardly even in use anymore) is a brace that attaches both on the jamb of the door and the door itself. These were the days before we had "pre-hung doors" in the lumber yards. It requires a router with a Dato bit set at a certain depth. When used correctly you end up with slots to fit the hinges into.

The proper way to set the jig is to align one end with the top of the Jjmb or the end of the top of a door. The correct distance off the floor for the hinges, coincides with the mark of thirty-six inches from the floor (standard height) for a door knob, which requires a different jig and tool. But in today's world it is all done in the factory and we call these "pre-hung." My father-in-law Milt taught me to use this jig, and in the case of no power available to do the same function from scratch using a sharp chisel. He taught me how to strike the chisel, how to plow with it, and edge trim so as not to cut too deep. Yes, it requires a set of very sharp chisels, which are a main staple for any master carpenter. I still guard well certain chisels suited for finish work, and they don't get used in place of a screwdriver or concrete tool, no way! I keep them sheatheded and protected, sharpened for use at specific times. Growing up in Rapid City, I was privileged to see the handmade "from scratch" doors my grandfather Arthur Hannant made in the 1940s. He owned a sawmill, and he also built several homes in West Rapid.

And now my on-the-job training is proving the God-given skill sets I inherited from my forefathers. Trims and finishes are like the icing on the cake, they are the eye-catching beautiful décor that makes a project stand out with clean lines and professional craftsmanship. Exodus 35:35 – "He has filled them with skill to do every sort of work done by an engraver or by a designer or by an embroiderer in blue and purple and scarlet yarns and fine twined linen, or by a weaver – by any sort of workman or skilled designer."

8. Maintain and Warranty

Psalm 97:10 – "Oh you who love the Lord, hate evil! He preserves the lives of the saints; he delivers them from the hand of the wicked." The term *preserve* in this Psalm carries several meanings useful for this next topic of maintenance and warranty. It also places the term in a context of guarding believers against evil behavior. Each client I have ever had insisted on quality workmanship and a guarantee of warranty for the work. This is a huge driver in keeping oneself from being influenced to anger, pride, covetousness, greed, or to be a door mat to every whim and want. If as craftsmen we do our job, it means warranty work is slim to nil, and maintenance is like the easy yoke our Lord promises. Make no mistake about it, though, the love of money is the root of all evil, and folks with the resources to build custom homes are thinking of their property as castles, not as houses. The mindset is enough to make any tradesman take pause before they measure or cut or place a board into position. This is a critical lesson for the novice to understand, your work and reputation will be preserved if you do it right the first time. *It takes longer to do it over than it does to do to right.* The idea of preservation is certainly manifested in the carpenter, but it is also a marvelous point to consider about God. God places the earth in such a position in the universe, on an axis, and at the perfect spot to avoid asteroids, yet be warmed by the sun without going to an extreme in temperature either way. God preserves gasoline, he preserves forests, oceans, birds, by his word. Man was created to maintain and preserve and to have dominion over all creation – we are co-partners with God. God does not call the qualified into service, He is the qualifier of the called who serve him. Again, like our Lord, this bivocational model uses the platform of the world to teach us His ways, and continue to mature in faith.

9. Word-of-Mouth and Reputation (including payments and accounting)

The most common method of sharing the gospel has always been "one-on-one," or one person at a time, and the words of the one who receives Christ are pure and true. Let your words be few. I Corinthians 14:19 – "Nevertheless, in church I would rather speak five words with my mind in order to instruct others, than ten thousand words in a tongue." Let your work speak for itself, and let the clients speak to one another to know the truth about you and your workmanship. Receiving a payment is the end of the matter and it represents an accounting close-out, other than depositing the payment in a bank. One of the most refreshing acts of service you can do is to do what you say you will do. Do it according to the account given to you before the project began, considering the parameters and need, and do it in a timely matter. One of my favorite methods of sharing my faith with a stranger is to use the Romans 6:23 passage: "For the wages of sin is death but the gift of God is eternal life in Christ Jesus our Lord." The coffee house models on the napkins offer a rough sketch of a canyon or space between God and people. The Gospel or cross/bridge becomes the avenue to speak to the client about the life-saving methods of the Lord. It can occur in three minutes, so you don't waste time with many words and it's easy to remember. Your workmanship does the speaking, and you will bore someone quickly if you take time to tell about what you do or have done rather than let your actions speak louder than your words. I typically do not advertise because it leaves room for God. God knows where he needs me next and I love relying on him because it builds faith.

10. Replenish Tools and New Client Search

Joel 3:10 – "Beat your plowshares into swords, and your pruning hooks into spears; let the weak say, 'I am a warrior.'" Micah 4:3 – "They shall beat their swords into plowshares..." Okay, so this appears to be a contradiction in scripture, but it cannot be and it is not. I believe the point here is that we need tools to do a job, and one smart accounting factor in the world of trade work is to replenish your equipment, sharpen the chisel, the knives, blades, saws, spears or whatever is needed to be ready for the next project. This is the fun part! Guys love to make up reasons to head to the tool aisle in a store and get the latest and greatest tools. Talk to any farmer and he will let you know that "iron" is key to getting the task done. Whether it is a plow, a tractor, a drill, a sword, or bow, we teach the novice to have the same opportunity as a professional and advantage he needs to become a professional. Client search has everything to do with going into the world and placing yourself at the disposal of God and the public.

It also has everything to do with your passion. Do you believe in your project or product? This must be taught because if you don't have a passion for what you do, then you will not come across well in your presentations to future clients. Is your passion strong enough to make you leave your comfort zone to make an appeal to a donor or client? Take a risk! My wife and I ventured into the world of fundraising in 2004, and trust me it was very humbling at first. But the more I am exposed to the missionary life, the more my definition of supporter or the definition of a client begin to meld into the same thing. Because of God's word, I understand that Noah may have built the ark, but the design and purpose was of the Lord. Solomon may have built the temple, but the reason for it and provisions came from the Lord. Nehemiah may have built the wall, but material came from a King and the purpose for the wall was to preserve a nation. Our clients are steppingstones to a great purpose, and recipients of the blessings of God. It's not just our hands to the plow. I therefore look at a clients as a supporting cast to a greater truth and purpose, to bring people to a knowledge of God and into a personal relationship with him. He loves us, He is crazy about us! We can be an answer to someone else's prayers when we walk in the Spirit.

11. Develop Partners and Form New Accounts (subcontractors and suppliers)

Exodus 18:13-23 tells how Moses greatly respected Jethro and received his family back from him. And while Jethro visited with Moses, he helped God's leader prioritize and delegate. Jethro's wise counsel proved to be a valuable lesson early in Moses's forty-year ministry of leading God's people. There are great examples in scripture I could give about the need for a counsel of tradesmen, ministry partners, and co-workers, and many are found in the book of Acts. As Hannant Construction developed and grew into a premier custom home company, I took example from the days of the Flaig Brothers who had great relationships with lumbermen and entrepreneurs. They worked with many important influencers in the City. By the time I began my own company, many of those influential names were gone, and I was starting out in an unknown territory. Who would be my partners?

The model I used to determine who they would be was simple: Can they provide material I need and can I trust them? Can I sit at counsel, smoke the peace pipe with them, gain their confidence, and them to me? Will they have my back when the going gets tough with a client? All I had to do was to create wonderful things with the material they provided. It was a beautiful relationship. In San Antonio, the same method has served me well. I have gone out of my way to meet new people and talk shop with seasoned tradesmen. It is so very important to have an outlet where you trust another operator in this business. And set calendars with future projects.

A Story Line: Marcelo Abarca Saez from Chile

I am Pastor Marcelo Abarca Sáez, married to Jocelyn Quiroga Aguilera, and with two children: Marcelo Israel and Paz Elisa.

I am forty-three years old. In 2000 we were ordained pastors of the Assembly of the Christian Church of Chile. In 2002 I went to study Law at the University of San Sebastián de Concepción, graduating in 2009. I maintain in this city a legal study that advises, preferably religious corporations, taking care of the solution of their legal conflicts.

As pastor, I minister to a church in the city of Quillón, in the Maule Region, and administrative activities are at the central level of my religious entity.

My life has been developed in a bivocational way, that is, performing two permanent tasks at once: one religious and one secular.

This experience has been enriching, and has allowed me to perform as a better person. The dynamic tension between legal advice to evangelical churches and the pastoral ministry demands a great effort, making the most of my time, and optimizing the use of my resources to give a satisfactory answer to all who demand a solution from me.

To all those ministers who exercise only the pastorate I give all my admiration and respect because, without a doubt, they are fulfilling God's purpose in their lives.

As for me, I have decided to express what I am in more than one activity. God has put more than one seed in my heart, which has generated different fruits for different people and needs. These vocations are an expression of my way of seeing life: as an endless number of activities and functions, but all of which have only one purpose: to fulfill God's will in me.

Jesus Christ was a lawyer, teacher, pastor, doctor, etc., and in only thirty-three years he was able to master the professions that form human hearts, giving them the design created by the Supreme Potter.

We are all builders of the Church of Jesus Christ. Some work efficiently in this work with only one tool; others, however, do it with two or more tools, according to how our God has allowed them to flourish. However, it is not about the number of tools we have for our work in the Work of the Lord, but the love and passion with which we fulfill the Great Commission: preach the Gospel of Salvation and make disciples.

In a deeper analysis, we are all bivocational, or rather multi-vocational, since no one can only be a pastor. Those of us who work for the Kingdom of the Lord know that we are also husbands, parents, counselors, musicians, cooks, teachers, and many more.

Faced with the discussion of whether it is better to have only one vocation, or to be bivocational, I think it is appropriate to state that both are welcome in ecclesial work; everyone, from our different perspectives, can contribute with the gifts we have received, to receive from Jesus's lips this statement: "Well done, good and faithful servant, you have been faithful over a little; I will put you over much. Enter into the joy of your master" (Mat 25:23)

REFINING GOLD

THE YEARS FROM 1968 to 2006 were a time of learning, teaching and application, of sound building process in the trades in my life prior to becoming a full time missionary to Mexico. There is nothing quite as exhilarating as learning a technique and then successfully putting it into practice. It is to this process I dedicate these principles taught to me by mostly God-fearing and experienced master craftsmen. The Lord has given me a passion to disciple others through the platform of my years in construction and missionary adventures. I'm praying my experience and words will be useful and will apply to your own contexts and applications. Our Lord Jesus was mentored by a carpenter (his earthly father, Joseph) as a young boy, and used building, construction, and financial ethics examples in His teaching method when He began His ministry. At the conclusion of His Sermon on the Mount, He gave us a sound building principle (Mt 7:24-26). David writes about the firm foundation God laid in Psalm 24:1,2. It is God's IDEA to REFINE us as we do the work we were created to do, for we are God's masterpiece (Eph 2:10). The raw material is already in our midst, around us in our own area of influence, which is the person of peace whom we can work with, waiting for a leader, a role model, or someone who will disciple them.

Romans 12 speaks of being transformed by the renewal of your mind; that by testing you may discern what is the will of God, which is already in place. Hebrews chap 11 underscores the idea that God has provided something better for us than what this world offers, and by faith we move forward into maturity. In keeping with my own instruction and making known to others that which I was taught, allow these antidotes from a book entitled *Exponential* by Dave and John Ferguson:[21]

- I do, you watch, we talk.
- I do, you help, we talk.
- You do, I help, we talk.
- You do, I watch, we talk.
- You do, someone else watches.

We must provide for our own house by way of instruction for our own members of the household, and be faithful to the process (1 Tim 5:8).

IMF (Idea, Model, and Foundation)

Discipleship/mentoring is like the beginning of a home building project, which starts with three basic principles: IMF (Idea, Model, and Foundation).

The First Principle in the IMF Illustration is Idea

As an owner/builder of Hannant Construction, I had the privilege of the first meeting with the customer/client with sketch book and pencil in hand. Ideas are born out of necessity or desire, the client has the need/want and a model house or image in mind, and they may or may not understand the steps in the process or the costs. A young man is asked to join a men's group in church and participate in a discussion on predestination. He has questions about the subject and must decide how he will begin to wrestle with it.

With my new client, questions arise, budgets are discussed, and plans are drawn (in pencil so they can be changed). The young man opens his mind and realizes that a deeper study is involved, authors and commentaries are chosen. Significant Bible discovery is beginning to unfold.

The client discovers aspects of context of location on the chosen ground for building. Will the house fit the context of the chosen ground? Will the model be conducive to family growth and personality? Will the foundation "rightly" be suitable to the terrain? The young man discovers a whole world of discussion between Calvinism and Arminianism and begins to understand where he can take an opinion and with whom he may side. We can get some idea of this in the parable of the SOIL in Matthew 13 where hearing the Word and retaining it is crucial to spiritual development. There are more ways than one in which a building project can go awry. Unless the young man commits his study time with the small group to prayer and seeks the Spirit for discernment, he may end up being confused. Unless stewardship is discussed and settled in the church construction process in the early stages, will the body of believers be able to afford the costs? Does the proposed budget fit their pocketbook? If not, some changes must occur in the very beginning to ensure a successful build? Unless the young man squares "idea" with scripture, "Where stands it Written?" Will he will ever hold and retain a right understanding of who he is in Christ? Essential to the process of discipleship is a willing person, a right and correct model, and a healthy foundation.

Jesus taught how to build, to do it on the rock, and called the man who hears His words wise (Mt 7:21-24). Verse 21 explains what the substance of the ROCK is "the one who does the will of my Father who is in heaven." The material or person we are looking for to apply the discipleship process is 1) a broken and contrite heart, 2) a willing servant, and 3) a person of peace, those who do the will of God! Three foundational principles in God's IDEA of discipleship are found below with corresponding scriptural references:

A. *Conversion process of the person:* John 3:16; Romans 5:8; Romans 3:23; Isaiah 64:6; Romans 5:12; James 1:14-16; Titus 3:5 Ephesians 2:8-9; Romans 6:23; John 1:12 Romans 10: 9, 13; 2 Corinthians 5: 17-18. A new creation in Christ (Born again).

B. *Keep the Commandments:* Matthew 22: 34-40, verses 37-40. TWO Commandments-Love the Lord your God with all your heart and with all your soul and with your mind. You shall love your neighbor as yourself and on these two commandments depends, all the Law and the Prophets. (Obedience as a mark of Maturity).

C. *Devoted Servants:* Acts 2:42 "and they devoted themselves to the apostles teaching and the fellowship, to the breaking of bread and the prayers" and James 2:14 (Devoted Servants).

Three main principles of IDEA are 1) Conversion or being born again, 2) demonstrating the commandment of Love, and 3) the devotion to God's Word. Lord I PRAY for the future servants and workers of the harvest, for the harvest is plentiful but the laborers are few (Mat 9:37).

Important warnings to the clients, new construction home-owners: Beware of the nature of the bond agreement between the builder and the client! If certain parts of the project are to be done by the owner/client, for example, then there are less guarantees and promises of satisfaction as well as timeframe expectation.

With the disciple and the teacher there must be an agreement of give and take, a commitment to each other to follow through with reading and writing, evidence of growth in the process, and willingness to learn.

With a contractor/client agreement, any changes in the plan would require a special compensation and amendment to the original agreement and promise. Should there be a problem with structural integrity, or with the ground conditions, or with payments, then work stops until the issue is confronted and dealt with. This is where our own personal wills muddle up the process to short-circuit things and reject the master's hand. Perhaps the teacher has compromised, or the student does, and soon the commitment levels begin to wane. The objective is to create a building that honors the builder and client that is within the cultural context. My personal goal in the process is to always do what I say I would do, to keep my word and teach my employees (or in this case future mentees) to do the same. Titus 2:1, 2 – "Teach what accords with sound doctrine, sober-minded, dignified, self-controlled, sound in faith, in love, in steadfastness and in sound speech." Likewise in 2 Corinthians 11:4 – "for if someone comes and proclaims another Jesus different from the one we proclaimed, or if you receive a different spirit than the one you received, or a different gospel than the one you accepted, you put up with it well enough but it will stifle." An old saying I grew up with in construction is "Too many cooks spoil the brew." It reminds me there is a lot of competition in the arena of ideas, and I would remind a client of mine to choose me or not, but once we get started, please honor the contract as I will or the result will be something less than our expectations.

Here is a practical example from my experience in Mexico as a church planting coach: One day during a Sunday school lesson I was teaching, I asked the members of the church to draw a picture of their idea of what a church looked like. The pastor's mother drew a picture of a grand Catholic-style cathedral with high bell towers. Most of the rest of the class did simple sketches of people helping people and read a Bible. My observation was that if this pastor was being influenced by his mother, would it affect the way he received my guidance? The answer was no in this case, but it reveals an inward human desire for brick and mortar grandeur. We discovered competition in the arena of ideas. I can appreciate architecture with an open mind, and at the same time don't rate it as high on my list of important characteristics of a healthy church. By the way, I built new and grand churches before my wife and I came to Mexico. Since then I have learned to soften and temper my excitement for structure and architecture with churches.

The Second Principle in the IMF Illustration is Model

In the DNA of discipleship within a church setting, every member must be committed and devoted to the needs of the community outside themselves and for the good of others. The model we/they choose for discipleship or for a church plant must also be a multiplication model. The idea expounded and acted on must be the "saturation of your territory" with communities of believers and discipleship-makers. The model should also include plenty of room for opportunity and grace in failure. Never give up, the stakes are very high, and the reward is heavenly and eternal. The model should constitute a significant amount of Bible discovery process used in the training of church planters. The Navigators have a strong plan of discipleship, for instance, a series called *Your Life In Christ* by NavPress, which is just the first of a seven-book series.[22] One model I used in Mexico is called the POUCH plan. It focuses on participative bible discovery and un-paid lay leaders. I understand there are many models to choose from, but the model needs to be in context with reality or the culture.

One of my favorite models for discipleship, and one that exemplifies the house-building process is taken from the Doctor of Ministry dissertation written by David F. Hunt to inform us about church planting in the Horn of Africa.[23] Again, in my past experience the process of building a home or a church includes not only "Idea and Model" but also Plan and Budget, Ground and foundation, Pre-Build and Delegate, Layout and Material, Dry-in and Infrastructure, Exteriors and Landscapes, Finishes and Turnkey, Maintenance and Warranty, Word-of-Mouth and Reputation, Replenish tools and Client search, Develop Partners and Form New Accounts, as described in the previous chapter. You can imagine the discipleship process as being one of great opportunity along the way for the novice who can perform in any of these areas according to his talent, teaching, and willingness (one body, many parts) and designed to serve all. So, what about the absolutes in church planting, the X-factors and cultural differences in our ever-expanding world of information?

These following "pieces and parts" from Hunt's dissertation are to be considered a comprehensive package, not a buffet. These should be used together, interdependently, because one won't work without the others. All must typically be present in a multiplication movement (see Ps 24:1,2; Ps 127:1)

- *NATURAL:* New Life comes from the inside and is a product of birth, not organizational (RO 12:3-8; 1 Cor 12:12-31; Eph 1:15-23).

- *HEADSHIP:* Obey the Word of God, Jesus as the head, not the pastor. Believers discover for themselves what the word of God says (Col 1:18, Eph 1:22).

- *HOLY SPIRIT directed:* The Holy Spirit guides and empowers, not an organizational connection to a denominational hierarchy. Refreshing spontaneity (Jn 15:28-16:15; Acts 13:2,3; 1Cor 3:9-17).

- *FULL PARTICIPATION:* Everyone participates, clergy-laity separation is removed. Leaders lead through influence, not positions of authority. The people are the ministers and provide content at gatherings because ALL have gifts (Eph 4:11-16; 1 Cor 14:26; 1 Cor 3:9-13; Exo 19:5,6).

- *ONE ANOTHERING:* Responsibility to serve one another, love one another, expressed in action and mutual edification, which is the primary purpose of meeting (Acts 2:42-47; Acts 4: 32-35; Heb 10: 24,25; 1 Jn).

- *LEADERSHIP:* Clergy-Laity dichotomies disappear in a community of believers under the headship of Christ and without human intermediaries. God provides special leadership gifts to the church disciple to help fulfill the purpose of preparing people for the work of the ministry (Mt 23:1-12; 1 Thes 2:7-16; 1 Pet 5:1-4).

- *SIMPLE*: Pretend a war is on and the church building burns down. What is left? What can you give up and still be a church? What should remain are the people, the Bible, and God. (Mt 18:18-20; Acts 2:46,47).

- *AUTHENTIC COMMUNITY*: Believers are together and have everything in common, they meet together every day. Organic nature and simplicity foster relational bonds and strengthen family (1 Tim 3:14, 15; 2 Cor 13:11; 1 Pet 3:8).

- *EQUIPPING CENTER*: Outpost for Kingdom expansion could be mobile and accessible online, but also in a church building. Reaching beyond yourselves, focusing on saturating entire regions with the Gospel witness and mission in mind (Eph 4:11-13; 1 Cor 14:26-31).

The Model must be in context and always leading with influence through face to face encounters with transformational attitudes. To contextualize is not to change the message but rather to apply to every dimension of one's personality and to all the relationships in one's life. For example, the Gospel seed sown in Palestine resulted in Palestinian Christians, when sowed in Rome, resulted in Roman Christians, sowed in Great Britain, resulted in British Christianity and when sown in America it resulted in American Christianity. Good tactics can overcome poor strategy, but bad tactics will wipe out good strategy-George Patton. But Caleb quieted the people before Moses and said, "Let us go up at once and occupy it, for we are well able to overcome it." Lord I PRAY for men like Caleb with a different spirit (Numbers 13:30).

The Third Principle of the IMF Illustration is Foundation

Jesus used examples of failure when anything but solid a foundation is used, and it will crumble or be swept away when trials come (Mt 7:24-27). In my years of construction experience, nearly half of my time was spent developing a solid foundation prior to building structures above ground. In housing, we used either block or poured concrete set on solid stable footing on compacted ground, below frost levels. In large churches or building structures, infrastructure was placed at the same time below ground (HVAC, plumbing, electrical, communications) after the compaction process. Compaction in geology is a process leading to the formation of sedimentary rock by the pressing of overlying layers of sediment. During the discipleship process of a believer, much care, cost, and effort go into preparing a disciple who in turn will make disciples or "rock solid believers" (Eph 4:12-14). So, a pre-process is needed before presenting the meat and potatoes to new milk drinkers. This requires spending time with a prospect (potential person to be discipled), living life and experiencing casual everyday living with them first or "relationship before impartation of information."

It takes $1,100 to mine, extract, and refine one Troy ounce of gold. Gold is reduced or precipitated or changed from a state of solution to SOLID FORM. An outside agent must cause precipitation to happen. This is to say we assume, and rightly so, that the raw material already exists, as I have noted earlier. In another study, I'd love to speak about our amazing habitat and environment so wonderfully created to sustain life. But that will be for another time. Suffice it to say, we have all we need to sustain life. The key is in the "layers of sediment" in a believer's life and journey. Each experience in the life of a believer is like a layer of sediment that can be "precipitated" or processed to bring out the refined gold. Precipitation always needs an agent to do the action, so we attribute this to the Holy Spirit who convicts and directs us and a godly earthly teacher. For our vision to grow keener and in compliance with God's will, we must submit to growth-producing treatments and maintain good spiritual habits (1 Pet 1:7). Daniel 12:10 – "Many shall purify themselves and make themselves white and be refined, but the wicked shall act wickedly. And none of the wicked shall understand, but those who are wise shall understand." So, the foundation is critical and we must be able to observe and discern if a person is ready to be trained and developed so they can handle with maturity the deeper and difficult things (Zech 13:9; Lk 6:40; Eph 4:23; Heb 8:10).

In summary, the foundational process in a believer's life is like the "refinement of gold." The writer of Hebrews urges us to leave the elementary doctrine of Christ and go on to maturity and not be sluggish. If we are wishy-washy, then hardly anything put on us will hold up to the tests that are coming and we will not be reliable. If the clay in the kiln has not been precipitated, then the work of art will be destroyed in the fire. The air pockets of resistance will react violently to the heat. LORD I PRAY for our strength to rise up as we wait upon you, and for refinement in our walk with you. I pray for the vetting process of these new disciples, that as trainers we can be sure not to throw our pearls to the swine.

Refined gold is a theme in the beloved anthem *America the Beautiful*: "May God thy gold refine, till all success be nobleness, and every gain divine."

Personal experience from my years in construction has taught me that shoulder-to-shoulder training is the most effective way to disciple. *I do, you watch, we talk*, and then *you do, I watch, we talk* is very effective.

MORE APPLICATION

Carpenters Local 1780 Story

DANIEL 1:8-16 IS A story of Daniel's faithfulness and obedience to his former instruction, an example of sound training and teaching being put to the test. At the end of ten days, Daniel, Hananiah, Mishaal, and Azariah were found to be in perfect health. They put into practice what they knew to be right and true.

In 1979, at the Local Carpenters Union hall in Las Vegas, Nevada, my brothers-in-law Mike and Steve and I were put to a test. Having just finished a million-dollar custom home, we were seeking further long-term employment in Las Vegas. The track home industry was not to our standards. We learned the hard way that if we were to survive this culture we would have to adapt, and this was our first year in this new culture. The three of us drove to the local union hall where we had it on good information that work could be found. The union representatives listened to the three of us proclaim our intent to become registered as "Journeyman Carpenters" and thus deserving the high pay classification we were seeking. All three of us were in our late twenties and we hardly seemed worthy of union's designation as masters of the trade.

They proceeded with their written exams, and after an afternoon of written and oral questions, we were admitted into the union with the designation of Master-Journeyman. None of us missed a single question, and in fact spoke in such mature ways that the Local 1780 Union was amazed at our skill and ability. You see, our training in South Dakota years before was extensive, shoulder-to-shoulder style teaching with at least a dozen masters who were unified on the process of teaching novices like we once were. Over a period, we were part of the team of tradesmen that resulted in the construction of nearly 1,500 homes. Each one of us were like interchangeable parts that could be used at any juncture of the building process. We had been tried and tested and proved. The Vegas union test was a "cake walk" or "easy trial" to us. In our careers during the subsequent years, all three of us have become teachers of novices in the trades and have become "journeyman makers" because of what we have been taught and put into practice.

The Danny story: Constanța, Romania, 1998

From the beginning when the opportunity arose to travel to Romania, back in 1998, the one question I asked myself was "Who can I disciple?" Who was going to be the artist that would receive a hand-built easel, which I made especially for this trip? Who would get twenty-five sheets of Bogus gray chalk paper and forty sticks of lecturer's chalk? You see, at that time I was a "chalk artist" telling bible stories with an artistic presentation in twenty minutes. It is an old art form used for years, and still is in some parts of the US and the world. Someone I prayed about meeting was going to be equipped, trained, and released to do something special in the Kingdom of God.

Trained by a godly woman named Mary Doscher, who was a chalk artist in Rapid City, South Dakota, I embraced the calling to chalk. She made it a point to share the gospel in bars, schools, clubs and yes, in church too. Mary was about to retire from doing this, so she gave me her show easel, a rather large and heavy contraption that required a station wagon or a pickup truck to transport. Further training came for me within a group of pastors called the Christian Magicians who met in Winona Lake, Indiana in 1987. I met several seasoned chalk artists like Gary Means, Marcel Rydzinski, Steve Axel, and other great men and women of God. I was a sponge and soaked up their words and methods, quickly developing my own style.

After I relocated my family to Colorado and then Nebraska, in the next few years chalking became more of a personal hobby to me. But one truth remained: Passing on this skill to other young artists always remained in my heart and soul. Now, as an elder and leader in the Sidney EFC, the opportunity to go to Romania during the Easter holiday and do a Gospel presentation at little Grace Church seemed very exciting to me! And yes, there was one young man, according to the missionaries who attended Grace Church, a student at the Bucharest Art academy named Danny, who could be trained to chalk for Jesus.

The team included Pastor Doug Birky, Randy Babcock, and me representing the Sidney church, and we went to do an Easter message at the time of the Greek Orthodox celebration in Constanța. Our week-long series of messages, music, and art in the church and on the streets was planned, and soon I was preparing for my workshop. The end justified the means so I started with two linoleum tubes eight inches diameter and fifty-two inches long that could fit the equipment into them, to go as checked bags to Romania. The drawing board had to fit into the tube as well, so a hinged contraption using piano hinges and quarter-inch plywood did the trick. The light bank, a simple bar with porcelain fixtures needed to be disassembled to fit into the tubes. The easel, lights and easel legs went into one tube, the twenty-five sheets (three feet by four feet each) of paper and the forty sticks (three inches long by one inch square) of chalk went into the second tube.

Pastor Doug and I practiced for six full drawing events. He was on the keyboards and I was at my easel. Randy was our trip planner and coordinator with logistics and people in Romania. I remember meeting Ken and Gene at the airport and the overnight stay at the EFCA headquarters in Bucharest. The two missionaries were concerned about our gear, particularly the art stuff. The only hitch we encountered on the train to Constanța was a slow down on the Danube River and armed guards boarded the train to do a spot check. Ken and Gene were quickly ripping off any labels that indicated USA or American Airlines from those tubes! About 2:30 AM we arrived in Constanța after a grand total of thirty-two hours traveling east from Denver. We slept, and when the sun rose it was Wednesday morning (we had left on Monday), and the day I met Danny.

As soon as Ken Merrifield introduced us, the chemistry was there and my new student and I could prepare for the week of drawings. He was quite talented and was a new believer (twenty-four years old) with a broken-world story. He carried a personal bitterness over a mugging by a couple of men on the streets of Constanța. As I walked with him, it was an opportunity to listen to his heart and then formulate a sort of counsel to him. Because he was an artist, I used the illustration of a potter's wheel and the work of the master potter forming and shaping the lump of clay. The master uses a goad, a knife, a spoon, water, his hands, or whatever else is needed or required to form the shape desired. "Danny," I said, "God does the same thing for us in our lives as we put on the mind of Christ. We have been created for a specific purpose during a specific time and according to The Lord's intentions. The Lord places us in situations that challenge us, shape us, temper us, and perfect us." I prayed with him and helped him to understand a little bit how he could move on and learn from this event and use it for good as Joseph claimed in Genesis 50:20 –"As for you, you meant evil against me, but God meant it for good, to bring it about that many people should be kept alive, as they are today."

I went to his home and met his family, and they wanted me to tell them about the American Indians, and of course being from South Dakota, I readily shared a story about the Ogallala and Lakota Sioux-. Danny gave me a portfolio of some of his work while in College, and I gave him the easel and paper and chalk. It was a fair trade, but I was the one who was most honored. We spent as much time as we could together, and I left him some chalking literature and my notes. He practiced with and cherished the equipment. But the goodbye was heart-breaking. It was the custom of the Romanian church to do a sendoff for brothers in Christ from the west. We arrived at the train station with our gear, checked in, got the tickets to Bucharest, and walked out to the platform. There were dozens from the little Grace Church waiting to say goodbye to us. It continued even as we boarded and took our berth and tried to settle in. As the train pulled away, I remembered the folk song we sang in church, and saw the many hands waving goodbye. We dropped our window and began waving as well, until the train was out of site. It was a very emotional time for me and I was in tears, in part due to the fact it was also my first overseas short-term mission trip. It reminds me of I Thessalonians 2:8 – "So, being affectionately desirous of you, we were ready to share with you not only the gospel of God but also our own selves, because you had become so very dear to us."

The Water Plants: Mexico City, 2010-2012

A survey of Latin countries that have sent missionaries out-of-country to foreign lands in 2006 placed Mexico as number two among all Latin countries, with 313 young souls. The number-one missionary-sending Latin country was Brazil, with over 3,000 per year. Apparently being a young believer in Mexico is very rare. And yet, when I met José Nolasco, a student of civil engineering at UNAM, I knew those odds were going to change. He was part of a group who called themselves Young Mexican Missionaries, and they were 200 strong and on fire for Jesus. José was a leader with vision and the heart of a pastor, which is why I introduced him to a few elders in the Mexico Free Church called the FIEL. This young, passionate missionary deserved all the coaching I could provide and as much opportunity as he could get. In August 2009, FIEL pastors and

American missionaries and myself introduced him to an abandoned work/mission near a large city metro station. The building became a church plant location called Iglesia Rey, and the community had deep needs, including insufficient pure drinking water at a decent price.

"Take care of my sheep" (Jn 21:15-17). Water is such a precious commodity in third world countries as well as in major cities like Mexico City. The idea of creating a micro-enterprise within a newly formed Church plant seemed doable to me. I never really considered the odds against success, and I never really listened to any voice that exclaimed "You can't do that!" The need is so great, yet so under-appreciated, that a thirst for pure water and a thirst for the Word of God are closely related, as is the need to train up men and women. Why not ere on the positive side of the odds?

Oh, I did the homework, the due diligence, and counted the costs. It took almost two years of study and research that included consulting the University of Notre Dame Economics Department. It was about three years into our term as RG Missionaries in one of the largest metropolitan areas in the world when we launched the water plants for two FIEL Churches called REY & Vida Abundante. The finances were raised and training was provided by Inmaculada, a Mexico City company that produces non-sand filtered (chemical filter) plants.[24] They also promote entrepreneurial development by teaching strategy, offering courses on operational details, providing technical support, inspection of filters, and re-supply of bottles and equipment. Of course, the one area of concern I had was in the area of "ownership" and who within the congregants would take this on and be malleable and teachable. I refer to the precipitation chapter in this book because not everyone will be capable of this challenge. That said, in time both plants have been used to further God's Kingdom, but not in the way I first envisioned.

The churches chose the larger tanks which, if run properly, can produce 600 graphons (four-gallon containers) of water per day. Rey Church benefits from an established location, but Vida Abudante suffered from distance to the plant issues. They both needed to solve the questions of "Who will do it? Who will go and make this project produce fruit?" In the case of the REY Church, there was a single woman with a daughter to raise who had her own tiny water plant three blocks away. She became a member of the REY Church, loves the Lord, and caught the vision. She eventually took over the REY production and used transients and sojourners to help her run the plant. Today they use it like a well-oiled machine as REY Church has become a sanctuary church for immigrants who are separated from family. This holistic ministry provides a vehicle for dignity, hope, love, and compassion – oh yes, and a revenue stream too!

The Vida Abudante project went south, literally speaking, as it was located in the southern part of Mexico City, miles away from the church location. It became a strain on the two couples who volunteered to run the plant. To make a long story short, one of the core couples ended up purchasing the plant after it was located on his family ground in Tlauhuac. Abja and his wife eventually joined another church who caught the vision of pure water in a very poor area and now today enjoy success. Abja supplements his welding job income with running the water plant. Their influence within this community is supported by the fact they also live here. When it comes to sharing the gospel, it is supported with trust due to the pure water plant that also provides drinking water at a low price. In both cases, the risk of failure existed only if a suitable "Timothy-figure" the novice would not accept the gift of life, liberty, and dignity. But I remained confident in the Lord and patient in my understanding of the culture. In developed cultures world-wide, a safe time margin is between two to five years for a new business to become successful. Why should we limit ourselves with expectations that can be unfair? I'm no farmer but do understand that when a seed takes longer to sprout, it is because the root system generally is more substantial and deeper. Someone took the time to work the ground and prepare it. The idea may be sound, but the ground we precipitate and cultivate will receive the seed in a much healthier way.

Alcance Victoria

In retrospect, Jesus selected blue-collar workers to further the Gospel, so why don't we do the same? James 1:27 – "Religion that our God the Father accepts as pure and faultless is this: to look after orphans and widows in their distress and to keep oneself from being polluted by the world."

The name of this Church translates as "Reach for Glory" in one of the most violent neighborhoods in Mexico City. The Benito Juarez district probably has the highest percentage of poverty and crime in the Federal District, which features more housing units than tall buildings. Apartment complexes are common, and one is home to 1,500 people, about five minutes from Alcanze Victoria. This small outpost church was formed by recovering alcoholics who began a micro-enterprise business of making bread for local chicken stands and restaurants. To be sure, this is a charismatic group of believers, with a pastor leader "Rondo" who is fearless with the Gospel. The focus of his ministry is to reach widows, orphans, and fatherless children living in the streets or within a domestic violence home/apartment in this barrio. They want to reach the children, to be their role models when the adults are AWOL with drug addiction. Campus Crusade for Christ or CRU made contact thru an acquaintance, and CRU connected with José Nolasco and our REY Church plant (that had not yet received their building in the Alvaro Obregon borough). I had been discipling José, grooming him for ministry to become a pastor when we got the chance to do an outreach event for Alcance Victoria. Members of the REY group, Cru, Karla (my wife) and I, put a team together to present the Gospel through music, art, clowning, and giving testimony under a big-top tent.

Our team arrived at the complex before dark, but the sky was turning darker. The first thing you notice at the entry gate are the two shrines: Our Lady of Guadalupe on one side, and Santo Muerto on the other. Both had many gift offerings of flowers and photos adorned around them. Literally, it was your choice of good and evil representing the Spirit world within this complex. It reminded me of the time I visited a temple in Constan□a, Romania in 1998 during the Easter festival time, and the priests stood by two separate candle holders in their full-dress garb. One priest gave you a candle for the living and a prayer, the other priest gave you a candle for the dead and a prayer. If you made it back to your home on foot without the flame going out, your prayer would be answered. The other thing you cannot help but notice at this complex of 1,500 people is the run-down camp appearance and hundreds of children playing in the filth. Oh yes, there were police sitting in their squad cars that looked like they belonged in a demolition derby with their missing headlights and bumpers hanging off, and smoke filled the air. I don't mean cigarette smoke, either.

The team broke off into groups. Clowns went door-to-door to announce a program at 8:30PM and the rest unpacked the gear and others set up the tent. It was a big tent, capable of covering 200 people, and we were going to need it. The women and children flocked to us, and what few men there were living in the complex watched from a front porch or window. But soon it began to rain, and the tent was not completed – there were still some key steel stakes to be driven into the ground to hold the three main masts. Rondo and I took the ropes of one of the masts and held it for thirty minutes in a pouring rain while others found enough stakes to drive into the ground to secure it. I became good friends with Rondo that evening, and he told me I must be a true missionary to stand with him in the rain to protect the women and children. I told him, "You are a good pastor to care for these people the way you do, and I am honored to stand by your side." Meanwhile, our team was passing out gospel tracts and marshmallow treats, first aid packets, water, and hugs. We finished our program with one single light bulb that lit the over two hundred in attendance, and we finished when the rain stopped. After we had packed up and were ready to depart, some of the people came forward and said, "We don't want the Santo Muerto Shrine here anymore!" At a minimum, we affected the ambiance, improved the spiritual outlook, and prayed for many needs. It was midnight before Karla and I got back home to our northern borough of Azcapotzalco about an hour-and-a-half away by train.

The BIVO model is easy to explain with the story of Alcance: shoulder-to-shoulder in the community, micro-enterprise, and gospel-centered relationships work well and produce results. In summary: The men at this AA (Alcoholics Anonymous) group turned to church, put their trust in Jesus, and broke the stronghold of addiction over their lives. They recognized the path of destruction and death in their barrios/colonias (the Benito Juarez borough or municipality), and how the youth were affected by the conditions. The group became entrepreneurial to first sustain their own needs but also to promote dignity for others seeking a skill to survive and thrive. The growth and recovery of this AA group did not happen in a vacuum. Many witnessed their journey and it gained favor and trust in the community for them. OIKOS.

STRATEGY VS IDEOLOGY

IN JUNE 2014, I was recalling my time in Acapulco, Mexico in a dream, when our team from RG responded to a natural storm crisis. The scene was a mess on Punto Diamante where debris was washed up on the shoreline. Even though the village infrastructure up further away from the water had been damaged, it mostly remained intact. It also has been established there for hundreds of years. The vision I had, the takeaway and the lesson that came to me is this reality: I envisioned remnants of sandcastles mixed in with the debris that had been built with great care only to have been washed away. They were of sand that can wash away – you know, here today and gone tomorrow – because they were not part of the local infrastructure, the infrastructure of local people and local context or OIKOS. An *untested strategy* is like an *ideology*. An ideology is a concept not proven in reality. Yes, maybe it has been tried somewhere, but is it the correct strategy for any context? What does last

longer, however, are relationships developed in real-time, shoulder-to-shoulder ministry life. For instance, our team helped a man dig up seventy or more palm tree plants after the storm. He had a real need, so we spent hours rescuing his tiny plants in order to save his business from being wiped out and destroyed by the flood waters. He also discovered a dry Bible on a shelf in a small

home/shack that had not been destroyed. Where there was still yet life in the plant, even though buried in the muck, there was hope, and this man knew it was a God sighting.

On that trip I also had the privilege to take three other men with me into a remote jungle area to check on a small church that had a hillside fall into the building. We dug for hours and got quite a bit of mud out, and they invited us to share a meal at the end of the day. The women cooked fish over an open fire and made some bread and set up a small plastic table in honor of the four of us. The scene was completed by their prayers of thanksgiving and our acceptance of their gift of fish tacos. Sadly, we left that afternoon not knowing if we would return, and we never did. It was deemed by leadership at the time on the grounds that this location was not going to receive any other aid from us. But let me tell you, we made a memory and I will not forget the honor of sharing a meal and hard work with believers in that jungle. Not only did we become the hands and feet of Jesus, we walked alongside the people during a big important event, and it changed our lives as well.

About five years into our ministry overseas, long before the Acapulco crisis, we came back to the States to share about our work and raise support. There was a certain man who had been following our progress as EFCAIM missionaries (as the mission used to be called) when we departed for overseas. His comment to me was "Barry, you have grown and matured. I see a different Barry today. Not that you weren't mature in 2004, but **something has changed** in you. Funny how this occurs when you decide to push all your chips to the center of the table and exclaim, 'I'm all in! God send me. Use me.'" His comment prompted a short answer from me (we have been immersed into a foreign culture and have been affected by it) and then a more thoughtful realization of a series of firsts for Karla and me. This list is not all inclusive but is part of a list I wrote about the things I have learned in Mexico: It was a first for...

- Joining a mission agency.

- Raising support.

- Selling our belongings and leaving home.

- Closing/stopping our income endeavors/careers and earning mode.

- Saying goodbye to family and friends not knowing if we would see them again.

- Purchasing a one-way ticket to a foreign country.

- Entering the world of language training.

- Experiencing the loss of two parents while on the field.

- Gaining a grandson but seeing him only once or twice in two years.

- Extending a tourist visa and processing it beyond the first 180 days while in-country.

- Renewing an American passport in Mexico City.

- Dealing with interpersonal relationships with fellow missionaries.

- Being without a car for two-and-a-half years.

- Dealing with culture shock.

- Subjecting ourselves to dentists, doctors and hairstylists in the Spanish language.

- Adjusting to new food groups.

- Learning the Mexican legal system: IMM, FM3, etc.

- Being robbed on an underground train/metro.

- Sitting in a police station filling out a report (by the way there is little or no justice in Mexico and criminals are rarely caught.

- Receiving a short-term mission team solo on our own as the missionaries in charge.

- Seeing Mexican nationals accept Christ as Lord and savior.

- Sponsoring a missionary trip of young Mexican Christians to go to another country (from REY church to Costa Rica).

- Walking onto Mexican Universities and sharing the Gospel (UNAM-IPN-Linda Vista, Tech Monterrey and others).

- Teaching ESL in a middle school in Tultitlan and other Universities.

- Working directly with an Orphanage.

- Planting two new churches from scratch.

- Purchasing a Mexican vehicle in the Federal District

- Getting seriously lost in the Federal District.

Yes, for sure I have changed. Of course, I have, because the creative life of God is always coming, always entering to refresh and enhance our lives. Just as Christ re-entered His Creation so we also consciously steer our lives into danger areas. We go there in person, not necessarily to start a church, or heal the sick, or sponsor a big campaign, but simply to bring the presence of Christ into that situation. You know that a person who is willing to merely put up with life becomes a manager or a bureaucrat, not a leader. A leader must be troubled and discontent and ask how can tomorrow be better than today? An artist must ask a similar question. He cannot be satisfied with the most recent project with his hands, he must have the notion of never being completely satisfied with his work. Remember one biblical principle is that while God never changes, we must. We must daily put on the mind of Christ. Go and learn. As Dan Allender said in *Leading with a Limp*, "God calls leaders to tell a story of redemption through their lives as they lead others in the redeeming story of God."[25]

The novice becomes the master through trials, and it is our role as founders, forefathers, and mature believers to guide them into maturity and readiness for their fruitful ministry. Did not Elisha accomplish twice the marvelous works than did Elijah his master? Elijah mentored a single disciple, Jesus mentored twelve and more, and so do we today have similar opportunity. Healing in our community begins when we do something, when we take a step. Nothing results from apathy or a do-nothing attitude. God honors RADICAL RISK and risk-taking faith. When arks are built, lives are saved. When soldiers march, Jerichos tumble. When staffs are raised, seas are parted. When lunch is shared, thousands are fed. And yet we want God to help us in our non-involved lives?

Jabez Prayer

Four things Jabez prayed for: 1) That God would bless him indeed. Spiritual blessings are the best blessings. God's blessings are real things, and produce real effects. 2) That He would enlarge his territory. That God would enlarge our hearts, and so enlarge our portion in Himself, ought to be our desire and prayer. 3) That God's hand might be with him. God's hand with us, to lead us, protect us, strengthen us, and to work all our works in us and for us, is a hand all-sufficient for us. 4) That he would keep him from evil, the evil of sin, the evil of trouble, all the evil designs of his enemies that they might not hurt, nor make him a Jabez indeed, a man of sorrow. God granted that which he requested.

But we live in a broken world that seems to repeat history, and there is nothing new under the sun.

In the book of Ezekiel, the Glory of the Lord leaves the temple. What caused the presence of the Lord to leave? Why does it leave us? When people stop listening, God departs. When people stop trusting, God leaves. Romans 1:21 – "For although they knew God, they did not honor him as God or give thanks to him, but they became futile in their thinking, and their foolish hearts were darkened." What can be known about God is obvious, plain to people because God has shown us. Yet, as I mentioned in the beginning of this book, there seems to be an exodus away from traditional church settings. God gives us up for our lusting, our longings, and dishonorable passions (Ro 1:26).

However, you and I as believers have a mandate to go into all the world and be witnesses to unreached people and groups. It's very clear these days in America that Sunday is a day of labor (not rest) for many restaurants, movie theaters, construction sites, hospitals, supermarkets, gas stations, casinos, and so on. These are the areas outside the church, and even in homes, where people are waiting for *you*. John 14:12,13,14 – "Truly, truly I say to *you*, whoever believes in me will also do the works that I do; and greater works than these will he do, because I am going to the Father. Whatever *you* ask in my name, this I will do, that the Father may be glorified in the son. If *you* ask me anything in my name, I will do it.

Vista

West of San Antonio on Tally road at the local firehall is where Vista Community Church led by Pastor James Mendoza used to meet for Sunday service. For years they have dreamed and prayed about a new building to be raised on their property in Castroville, Texas. The pastor and I know each other from the FUEGO conference in 2013, a joint Navigator/ EFCA meeting. Pastor James loved to talk about their vision, and especially about their plans for growth and

expansion in western Bexar County. With my background, it seemed plausible that the nudge to help them achieve their plan would fit what I was feeling from the Holy Spirit. There was enough interest for me to accept a meeting with the Vista Elders to get some basic information on paper from Ken B. After the meeting, it occurred to me I could be a resource and a consultant for them, triggering a name for my new adventure: SBIC: San Antonio Bible Institute Consultant.

I met Ken in his office, and we discussed a building plan he showed me for an 8,000 square-foot single story metal building. When he asked me if I could accomplish their project, I shared with him an old blueprint (a cover sheet only) from the Dubuque, EFC project which was a 66,000 square-foot addition. This was my last stateside build with BCDG prior to going to the mission field. He looked at me and said, "Oh, okay yes, our church build should be no problem for you." The Vista Community Church has had a vision for the Castroville area for years, noticing how the natural push of the metropolitan San Antonio area had been migrating their way. I became part of their building committee and began doing "take-offs" or pricing and the size of building, with groundbreaking in the spring of 2018. The other element that soon came to be a reality was the bivocational element. Did I just candidate with a new supporting church as a missionary and agree to assist them in their building need? Yes, and this is a manner or way to be relevant in today's culture with fundraising and support as a missionary. Vista just joined my support team, but in return for a service. As I have been saying, this bivocational model places an apostolic missionary pastor directly in front of many who don't have a relationship with Jesus. I met men who did not know the Lord, prayed with them, worked beside them, and counseled them as well.

And just as important, while I would step into the gap and meet all the trades and oversee the work project, I also would get to train a couple of men who God brought me to disciple. Gus and Jorge became the first to experience my teaching while on the field of battle (on-the-job training) but with a Christian mentality and purpose. Pastor James himself introduced me to Gustavo, and when I met Gus, he and I agreed to a trial run. Well, Gus (as a novice carpenter) has stayed with me now beyond the Vista job, praise the Lord! Jorge worked more as a laborer. Both men came to me at a needy time in their lives, both speak Spanish, and both became my close friends. The Vista Church opened for business on FM471 between Thanksgiving and Christmas in 2018, and they doubled their congregation size. Already they are making plans for Phase Two of their land development! The Lord is good all the time. The BIVO model proves to be a viable choice for churches in a new way, and benefiting many in ways only God can orchestrate.

Hebrews 3:1-6 – "Therefore, holy brothers, you who share in a heavenly calling, consider Jesus, the apostle and high priest of our confession, who was faithful to him who appointed him, just as Moses also was faithful in all God's house. For Jesus has been counted worthy of more glory than Moses-as much more glory as the builder of a house has more honor than the house itself. For every house is built by someone, but the builder of all things is God. Now Moses was faithful in all God's house as a servant, to testify to the things that were to be spoken later, but Christ is faithful over God's house as a son. And we are his house if indeed we hold fast our confidence and our boasting in our hope.

#31

BIVO is perfect for this type of ministry because of the potential proving ground for laymen and novice helpers. To be honest, the first thing I needed was a seasoned crew to initiate the groundwork and get the foundation in place. KC Jones and his men were hardworking brothers and I used a group of steel tiers from SE San Antonio as well as other professional concrete placement crews. The Ingram Plant brought their first ten-yard truck at 4:30AM and twenty-nine more followed all morning long. By sunrise we had

300 yards laid and the men were ready for a break. Fifty-four men needed tacos and hot sauce, so I sent Archie to the local taco place to get breakfast for the crew. At one point there were about a dozen men in front of me, so I engaged in simple dialogue about the Lord. I informed them they were working on a new church and asked them if they had a church they attended. Most of them said no, so I invited them to return to this one because they would be very welcome. I reminded them they had a hand in the answer to Vista's prayers to reach the community with this new tool.

Tertullian was an early Christian writer of who explained the unpalatable truth that "the Church is not a conclave of bishops, but the people of the Holy Spirit."[26]

I remember during team meetings in Latin America the illustration of building a plane while it is in flight. The idea at the time was reflecting change in policy as the city teams continued to engage their respective culture. And here is a famous author, Tertullian, teaching once again that there is nothing new under the sun. It's a no-brainer! Holistic ministry bathed in the Spirit builds up and edifies the kingdom of God.

Al Blake

During a summer of restoration projects in the Badlands of South Dakota and at the Manderson School District east of Rapid City, I shared the gospel with Al Blake. Mousel Construction (an A-8 government contractor owned by a woman of Oglala Sioux descent) had contracts with a Reservation School District and a Badlands nature trail and dumping station for RVs (tourist locations). Mousel placed five men on those projects, including me, who were employees, foremen if you will, to oversee Indian labor to perform the projects. I became a teacher and trained some of the more adept helpers who showed skill and ability. Al became a sort of a referee for us when trouble occurred between the Indians.

There was an incident at the six-room schoolhouse when I was teaching four young men to paint the with block filler the inside walls of each classroom. It got out of hand when one of them hurled a roller and extension handle full of paint at an Oklahoma Indian who was not welcome among the Sioux. Painting got out of hand when they decided to make hand prints on the walls, and then turn on each other with a paint fight. Al was a key element in breaking up the rivalry and roughhousing.

The daily routine was that our Rapid City Crew met at pre-dawn at the Mousel shop to get the company trucks and load supplies, then drive to the RV dump station work site. My companion for about three months was Al Blake. Al was the type of man who was as rough as they come, wore the same clothes all week, was a bit overweight, chewed tobacco all day long, and had a Santa Claus kind of laugh. He was our team laborer, runner, and all-around utility guy. So, what do you talk about on an hour-and-a-half drive to a remote location in the badlands with a man like Al? He was good with the children, knew the Ogallala culture and landscape, and his family was Catholic. Al, for some reason, did not attend church with his family and he had questions about God. He did not wish to become a Catholic. Meanwhile, my own faith was growing, I was being nurtured in the Word, and it was a time of significant Bible discovery for me.

The Lord placed me with Al to talk about Jesus, the Apostles, and miracles we found in the Bible. Al was my sounding board, and he amazingly responded with keen insight and genuinely loved our conversations each morning. One morning after the ground had been tilled (spiritually speaking), the Spirit led me to realize Al was ready to accept Christ as his savior. I shared the believer's prayer with him and he repeated every word, and even with tears.

At the RV station project, not far from Wasta and a famous place called Wall Drug, we waited for a cement truck to spin more water into the mix. As the ten-yard truck was brimming with speed and spinning around, Al was leaning on his shovel and let out a yelp! He grabbed his chest and yelled, "Oh shit"! Right then and there ol' Al (fifty-eight years old at the time) fell dead of a massive heart attack. Mike Heller and I called for backup to the Army Corps Engineers station and proceeded to perform CPR for forty-five minutes. Finally, the ambulance arrived but Al was already gone. Some of the workers just sat and wept on the dirt bank, but we still needed to lay down the concrete that could not be wasted. By the time all the dust settled, it was nearly sunset as we drove back to Rapid City. As per the wishes of Al, his family did not do a funeral at the Catholic church. Instead, they chose the funeral home and a protestant minister to perform the ritual. Our entire crew from Mousel Construction sat in two rows as Al's wife and son were escorted in. The director of the funeral told her they were Al's Co-workers and we began introducing ourselves. When she heard my name, she opened with a smile and asked me to step out into the aisle for a big hug. Then she asked me to say something for and about Al. "For you see, Barry," she said, "I know he was a believer. Al shared about every one of your talks with him."

The director sat me and Tony, Al's son, up front and we waited for our roles in the service. But when it came time, Tony could not control himself from emotion and tears and stayed sitting while I comforted him. The minister then began to close the proceedings and mentioned we would all meet graveside. But it was not over yet. A woman got up in front, turned around, and introduced herself as Al's sister who lives in California. She said, "I know Al is in Heaven right now because Al believed in Jesus as his savior. I know this because of the letters Al sent me about his faith and how he has walked with our Lord. And I am very sure that if Al could speak this morning, he would let you all know that you need to have personal relationship with Jesus."

Amen! I introduced myself to his sister afterwards, and what a blessing it was to speak with a fellow believer (a sister in Christ) you have never met. It's as if you have known them for ages.

Perhaps the story about Al, more than anything as a tradesman in my journey with the Lord, is my deepest purpose to write a book called *The Hammer and the Pulpit.* Yes, I get excited about the trade work, artistically speaking, but more than this it puts me in unreached areas where normal people need hope. They need Jesus, just like the man in the forest I met one morning while gathering pinecones.

In the forest above the borough or municipality Cuajimalpa, Mexico City, there is a sanctuary where the early monks built a monastery in the center of the "Desierto De Los Leones." This is a historic landmark and is located on the Highway to Toluca at a higher elevation than Mexico City, approaching **8,000 feet** above sea level. In fact, the Mexican Olympic track and field team practice at this higher elevation. It is a legendary location where, at one point in history, the black puma roamed free, but for some reason it was considered a desert-like place. Therefore, the name in Spanish was formed. It was also a refuge for the famous outlaw Emilio Zapata who favored the men and women who worked the soil and produced crops from the land. The trees in this forest are tall like redwoods but smaller in diameter, and they produce a rather large pine cone up to fourteen inches long and up to four inches in diameter. This cone is full of sap that is a perfect fire-starting fuel for

IT IS GOD *who has made us.* II COR. 5:5   BFH

the many wood fireplaces in the homes found near the national park. Our missionary home for a while was nestled near this forest in a community called Santa Rosa Xoxiac, with a spectacular view of nature and Mexico City. I would take a break from the activity of being a missionary and hike to the top of some of the ridges in this forest with black garbage bags, gathering fallen pine cones for the two fireplaces in our rustic mountain home.

I took the Pathfinder up into the deep forest for about four miles from our place and found a clearing to park it. As was my custom, I carried a walking stick, a pocket knife (Leatherman), a bottle of water, and a couple of black garbage bags and, just in case, my Spanish Bible on the front seat of the car. Yes, this was sup-posed to be a day of rest, a JAM day, meaning "Jesus And Me," with no expectation of an encounter other than fresh air. I mean, every day we entered the city transportation routes, metros, streets and so on to go and be the hands and feet of Jesus. How about a little quiet time out here to be refreshed by the woods? As I left the vehicle, out of the corner of my eye I saw a man stepping through the trees into the clearing where I was parked. It was he and I, in the middle of the forest, my senses warning me to not stick around but instead look for a quiet place of solitude undis-turbed by anyone else.

So, back to the Pathfinder I went and I pulled away to drive another mile up the road to a wide spot and parked again. I climbed for an hour, filled two bags with pine cones and dragged them back down the ridge to the vehicle. I grabbed a drink of water and proceeded to make my way back down towards the village area. I passed the clearing where I met the stranger earlier, and around the next bend in the road he was sitting on a stump ahead of me. This time, I got a nudge to stop and asked if he needed a ride back down the hill. Yes, was his answer, and he seemed very grateful.

After five minutes of conversation it was clear to me, he needed to hear the gospel. Again, we found another wide spot in the road, and pulled over and got out my bible. The man was a spiritualist, a "dreamer poet" of sorts, and his worldview did not match what I know to be God's Word on creation, our soul, and purpose for life. He lived in the village below my place and walks to this secluded location to be re-filled with nature. It was a perfect opportunity for me to share about the case for the Trinity, the creation, and a relationship (not a religion) with God.

I spent a good hour with him, and eventually encouraged him to ask Jesus into his life. It all seemed like a risk to me. Maybe I should have let him go and not stopped for that second encounter, BUT GOD gave the nudge to speak with this stranger, so I used God's words. Can I tell you any more about how this man used the good news? I cannot, because I never saw him again. Whatever decision he made it was with God and I was only the messenger. As a former co-worker of mine once said, "The plan is, the plan will change" (thanks, Eric). My JAM day turned into a testify-about-Jesus day. And I was more blessed by the encounter. And to finish with an important takeaway: You never know if you will ever see some people again. It is an unwritten concept in a city of millions that the one time you do meet and converse with a stranger is your last opportunity to share with them. In some ways it is disheartening because this side of heaven we don't know the eternal fate of those we encounter.

Be partakers, not takers. Get involved in the heavenly calling of the Spirit to share the grace that comes from heaven. Christians are called into the darkness to bring a marvelous light that has the power to affect the souls of men, to have a conversation that prepares them to live forever with God in heaven. I think we can think too little of Jesus in terms of not often enough in our daily routine. If, by our habit,s we can increase the chance of deeper acquaintance with him, then we benefit through the working-out of our faith through sanctification. This world we live in was made ex nihilo or out of nothing, but the church is made from materials at times unworthy or unfit for such a building. I pray for bold and open profession of the truths of the gospel, upon which our hopes of grace and glory are built. Our actions can and do speak louder than our words. Be courageous and walk by faith.

GATEWAY (GW)

The EFCA Theological Institute is where many men and women, pastors, immigrant and urban leaders, church planters, second-career people, church leaders, and members receive theological training to help prepare them for further ministry. Some students are also using this training to help prepare them for the Evangelical Free Church of America credentialing process. I am a GATEWAY facilitator, able to teach in both Spanish and English, and I serve all seventeen districts of the EFCA.

Matthew 5: 13,16 – "You are the salt of the earth, but if salt has lost its taste, how shall its saltiness be restored? It is no longer good for anything except to be thrown out and trampled under people's feet. In the same way, let your light shine before others, so that they may see your good works and give glory to your Father who is in heaven." I am not a fatalist in my thinking, nor do I look at a glass as half empty because it is also half full. We strive for our cup to run over, do we not? The question therefore is not rhetorical or without a positive answer or response. Yes, we can grieve the Spirit. Yes, we can fall away in our walk. Yes, we can become "luke warm," but this remains a choice we make, not God. This question put to us by Jesus in Matthew 5:13 is about losing the salt in us, and is also addressed in Mark 9:50 – "Salt is good, but if it loses its saltiness, how do you make it salty again? Have salt in yourselves, and be at peace with one another." Notice there is an answer to the question, and it has to do with shoring up theology in the hearts of men and women on the field of ministry. Notice as well we are told in Mark 9:50 to have salt, and to be at peace with others. It fits very well with a BIVO mentality, which is to be in good favor with both God and man. This pleases God.

GATEWAY is a tool to maintain salt and light, a structure to help the laymen in our churches, which are the pastors already working in enemy territory, and to continue to show their light. I was first introduced to GW while in the field in Mexico, with no time to stop the church planting and holistic ministries Karla and I were doing. It became a perfect vehicle for active laymen other than the LAP training I had done with Al Tunberg through the EFCA. GW for me needed to be done in Spanish, so I went through the year-long course with Mexican leaders side-by-side, shoulder-to-shoulder. It was not easy for me to think in Spanish rather than English, but I was carried along by the Spirit and did overcome the challenge. I needed to read Wayne Grudem and Evangelical Convictions books in English and Spanish. These books are heavily marked up with page references leading me to the interpretations I needed with some parts of theology. I was being trained by the Spirit to gain a skill set to be of good use for stateside GATEWAY students who prefer Spanish GW classes over English. The BIVO model works as a preserver like salt, and helps us keep our light shining in the darkness.

Furthermore, it places me in a position of being able to empathize with our Hispanic brothers and sisters with the challenges of language. By the way, I highly recommend you study the way verbs of expressions treat certain theological understandings. For instance John 1:4/Juan 1:4 "En El estaba la vida, y la vida era la luz de los hombres." The ESV states the same verse this way: "In him was life, and the life was the light of men." The difference can be unpacked like this: The verb *estar* in Spanish is conjugated to indicate a time line. The written word "estaba" tells the reader this was an action that occurred in the past but has also not been completed yet. The Hispanic student can then be deeper enriched with a verse such as Hebrews 13:8 – "Jesus Christ is the same yesterday, today and forever." Even more interesting are the well-known Latino writers, musicians, artisans, builders, and engineers who grace our world with color and flavor in everything they set out to accomplish. Can you imagine what it would have looked like if Latino engineers could have assisted the Hattians in their building processes to ensure stronger foundations and walls? Both countries are in designated Zone 2 or earthquake zones. In Mexico City alone the genius designs incorporate shock absorbers in their footings. If there could have been Christian builders in Haiti during the 1980s, maybe there would not have been so much loss of life after the terrible quake in 2009.

BIVO pastors strive to make things, people, and places better than when they first encountered them.

In 2016-2017 there were eleven Hispanic students in Storm Lake/Alta, Iowa who began a GW class. While not all of them passed the course, the impact this group made on the expansion of the church is unquestionable. Pastor Renato, Jimenez led his laymen into this GW course because he recognized they needed to gain alignment and refinement of their faith. People need to know how to defend their faith. People need to learn how to better articulate their belief systems.

Albert Cruz attended this class, but did so while living in another town away from Alta and is a leader of the Hispanic growth there. Elsa Flores is a wonderful matriarch, a Mexican Mama with tremendous influence on her people, and she grew so much stronger and full of salt and light during this class. Gabriela "Gabby" Rosales, perhaps the hardest-working student, struggled to complete the assignments and did burn her candle overtime to get the papers written. Guadalupe Carrillo was the quiet leader/poet in the group with a dark secular background, and he was also the newest believer in the group. His writings are indicative of the Hispanic flair and color I spoke about, and being aligned with the EFCA gave him even more courage to become pastoral. I so loved this group that when it came time for them to receive their certificates, I went in person to do it. The Summit Church was very proud of the spiritual growth demonstrated by this group, and they held a special ceremony in a Sunday service for the presentations. The clapping and cheers of congratulations from the over 300 present was an exciting event for all of us. Gabbycommented to me afterwards, "Barry, this is the biggest accomplishment of my life."

So, there it is: GW and BIVO are designed to put tools in people's hands and teach them how to properly use the tools of life (get busy living or get busy dying). My next challenge is to facilitate a Spanish GW for six pastors in the Texas-Oklahoma EFCA District, and each one is already launching a church plant. Psalm 133:1 – "Behold, how good and pleasant it is when brothers dwell in unity!"

As I mentioned at the beginning, I believe the two biblical passages encouraging, even mandating bivocational ministry, include Luke 2:52 and Matthew 3:16,17 about being in good standing with both men and God. Returning to these scripture verses brings this writing to a fitting close or, should I say, to a fitting beginning, because now it's your turn! Learn how to be in good standing with both men and God because this pleases God.

Barry F Hannant
June, 2020

NOTES

ENDNOTES

1 https://www.efca.org/ministries/reachnational/efca-gateway

2 https://en.wikipedia.org/wiki/
The_Agony_and_the_Ecstasy_(novel)

3 https://www.churchdevelopment.net

4 https://en.wikipedia.org/wiki/MacGyver

5 https://www.amazon.com/
Work-Matters-Connecting-Sunday-Worship/dp/1433526670

6 NEED REFERENCE FOR LIVINGSTONE STORY

7 https://www.amazon.com/
Evangelism-Outside-Box-People-Experience/dp/0830822763

8 https://www.efcatoday.org/story/church-history-bivo

9 https://www.amazon.com/
Total-Church-Radical-Reshaping-Community/dp/1433502089

10 http://www.garythomas.com/books/authentic-faith/

11 https://www.amazon.com/
Oneness-Embraced-Through-Eyes-Evans/dp/0802417906

12 REFERENCE?

13 http://www.evolutionofacreationist.com

14 https://en.wikipedia.org/wiki/When_Helping_Hurts

15 https://en.wikipedia.org/wiki/Richard_Arkwright

16 https://en.wikipedia.org/wiki/Vasco_de_Quiroga

17 https://www.kingdomaircorps.org/king-ranch

18 https://www.christianitytoday.com/edstetzer/2010/june/
    whatever-happened-to-gospel-leadership-book-inter-
    view-with.html

19 https://www.amazon.com/
    Whatever-Happened-Gospel-David-Nicholas/dp/1615071547

20 https://watermission.org

21 https://www.amazon.com/Exponential-
    Friends-Missional-Church-Movement/
    dp/0310326788

22 https://www.navpress.com/p/classic-design-for-discipleship-bi-
    ble-studies-1-your-life-in-christ/9781641582124

23 https://www.simplechurchrevolution.com/down-
    loads/2009huntcpmdissertation.pdf

24 https://www.aguainmaculada.com

25 https://theallendercenter.org/store/products/
    leading-with-a-limp/

26 http://www.tertullian.org/readfirst.htm

Lightning Source UK Ltd.
Milton Keynes UK
UKHW020218101120
373078UK00007B/327

9 781631 299841